Start Your Own

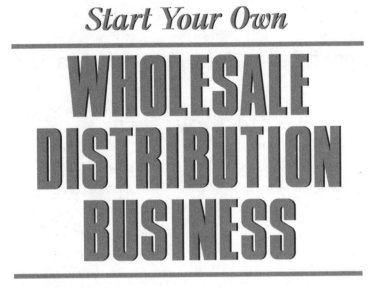

WHOLESALE DISTRIBUTION BUSINESS

D0746567

Additional titles in *Entrepreneur's* Startup Series

Start Your Own

Entrepreneur MAGAZINE'S

startup

3RD EDITION

Start Your Own

WHOLESALE DISTRIBUTION BUSINESS

Your Step-by-Step Guide to Success

Entrepreneur Press and Bridget McCrea

EP
Entrepreneur
PRESS®

Entrepreneur Press, Publisher
Cover Design: Beth Hansen-Winter
Production and Composition: Eliot House Productions

This publication is designed to provide accurate and authoritative information in regard to
the subject matter covered. It is sold with the understanding that the publisher is not
engaged in rendering legal, accounting or other professional services. If legal advice or other
expert assistance is required, the services of a competent professional person should be
sought.

Library of Congress Cataloging-in-Publication Data
McCrea, Bridget.
    Start your own wholesale distribution business: your step-by-step guide to success / by
Entrepreneur Press and Bridget McCrea.
        p.   cm.   — (Start your own)
    Revised edition of the author's Start your own wholesale distribution business, pub-
lished in 2006.
        Includes index.
    ISBN-13: 978-1-59918-545-3 (alk. paper)
    ISBN-10: 1-59918-545-8 (alk. paper)
        1. Wholesale trade. 2. Entrepreneurship. I. Entrepreneur Press. II. Title.
HF5420.M33 2014
658.8'60681—dc23   2014025086

Printed in the United States of America

18 17 16 15 14   10 9 8 7 6 5 4 3 2 1

Contents

Preface

Thinking back to my first "real" job, I remember walking into a small showroom full of welding supplies and miscellaneous products hanging on pegs and wondering to myself, "What in the world does this company do?"

At the time, all I knew about a welding supply distributorship was that it paid well compared with the rest of the jobs I had interviewed for, and the owner seemed slightly impressed with my resume. With that, I found myself in the position of office manager for a three-person wholesale distributorship. My duties included loading trucks bound for job sites with cylinders of welding gases, packing and shipping boxes of welding wire headed overseas to companies like Air Products, and delivering damaged hydraulic gauges to a repair shop for a local cryogenics plant.

What followed was four years of hands-on experience in the wholesale distribution business. When I became a freelance business journalist, that job experience stuck, and I landed various distribution- and industry-related assignments.

Today the distribution landscape is a bit different than it was back in the early '90s, when I was filling out government bids for welding machines. Between rapid advances in technology and the most recent economic recession, the wholesale distribution landscape has gone through many changes. Add in the fact that huge, online-only retailers like Amazon have moved into new wholesale product categories and it's clear to see that today's distribution landscape is very different than the one that company's operated in back in the '90s and '00s. The good news—as you'll read in this book—is that there are still many opportunities for wholesale distributors to carve out their niches in the business world. The fact is, manufacturers couldn't survive without distribution networks. Sure some of them may opt to sell "direct" (i.e., creating their own sales networks to sell directly to customers), but for the most part the firms that develop and market products need the help of wholesale distributors to get their products to market.

Take the electrical distribution sector, for example. I regularly interview both manufacturers and distributors for *The Electrical Distributor* magazine, and both sides preach the value that distributors bring to the table. So even in a world where the next product source is just a click away on the internet, the knowledge, expertise, and customer service that a wholesale distributor provides remains a strong component of any manufacturer's go-to-market strategy.

On the other side of the coin, the companies and other organizations that buy from distributors are also highly dependent on these expert middlemen. No manufacturer in the world can give the proper amount of attention to every end user. However, when territories are broken down and covered by individual distributorships, the task suddenly becomes more manageable. Take the contractor stuck on a job site in need of technical assistance with a product just purchased through a local distributor. Who do you think he should call—the distributor or the manufacturer? One is local, while the other will probably require a long-distance call and some time spent on hold.

In the end, it doesn't look like the wholesale distribution industry is going to be phased out by direct sellers and buyers who no longer want to deal with a middleman anytime soon. You'll meet all the entrepreneurs and experts we interviewed and you'll see the industry is thriving. Plus, manufacturers will always rely on distributors to act on their behalf when it comes to functions such as customer service, sales, collections, and marketing.

I hope this book assists you in realizing your dreams of entrepreneurship. Good luck in your ventures.

Introduction to Wholesale Distribution

So you want to start a wholesale distributorship. Whether you're currently a white-collar professional, a manager worried about being downsized, or bored with your current job, this may be the right business for you. Much like the merchant traders of the 18th century, you'll be trading goods for profit. And while the romantic notion of standing on a dock in the dead of night haggling over a tea shipment may be a bit far-fetched, today's wholesale distributor is a descendent of those hardy traders who bought and sold goods hundreds of years ago.

The Distributor's Role

As you probably know, manufacturers produce products and retailers sell them to end users. A can of motor oil, for example, is manufactured and packaged, then sold to automobile owners through retail outlets and repair shops. In between, however, there are a few key operators—also known as distributors—who serve to move the product from manufacturer to market. Some are retail distributors, who sell directly to consumers (end users). Others are known as merchant wholesale distributors; they buy products from the manufacturer, or another source, then move them from their warehouses to companies that either want to resell the products to end users or use them in their own operations.

According to the National Association of Wholesale-Distributors (NAW), wholesale trade increased by 5.8 percent in 2012 (compared to the prior year) with sales reaching $4.9 trillion. "The year was not without challenges, but it was a profitable year for adequately prepared wholesaler-distributors," NAW reports, noting that wholesale trade employment averaged 5.7 million workers in 2012, a gain of 1.8 percent over 2011. NAW says wholesale trade itself accounts for about 5.6 percent of U.S. GDP and is an integral part of other larger sectors of the economy—retail trade and manufacturing (source: www.naw.org/about/industry.php). That's a big chunk of change, and one that you can tap into with the help of this book. The field of wholesale distribution is a true buying and selling game—one that requires good negotiation skills, a nose for sniffing out the next "hot" item in your particular category, and keen salesmanship. The idea is to buy the product at a low price, and then make a profit by tacking on a dollar amount low enough that it still makes the deal attractive to your customer.

Experts agree that to succeed in the wholesale distribution business, you need to possess a varied job background. Most experts feel a sales background is necessary, too, as are the people skills that go with being an outside salesperson who hits the streets or picks up the phone and goes on a cold-calling spree to search for new customers.

In addition to sales skills, the owner of a new wholesale distribution company will need the operational skills necessary for running such a company. For example, finance and business management skills and experience are necessary, as is the ability to handle the "back end" (those activities that go on behind the scenes, like warehouse setup and organization, shipping and receiving, and customer service). Of course, these back-end functions can also be handled by employees with experience in these areas if your budget allows.

"Operating very efficiently and turning your inventory over quickly are the keys to making money," says Adam Fein, president of Pembroke Consulting Inc., a Philadelphia strategic consulting firm. "It's a service business that deals with business customers, as opposed to general consumers. The startup entrepreneur must be able to understand customer needs and learn how to serve them well."

According to Fein, hundreds of new wholesale distribution businesses are started every year, typically by ex-salespeople from larger distributors who break out on their own with a few clients in tow. "Whether they can grow the firm and really become a long-term entity is the much more difficult guess," says Fein. "Success in wholesale distribution involves moving from a customer service/sales orientation to the operational process of managing a very complex business." Luckily, the book in your hands will help take the guesswork out of this transition by giving you the tools you need to succeed.

Getting Into the Game

Wholesale distribution firms, which sell both durable goods (furniture, office equipment, industrial supplies, and other goods that can be used repeatedly) and non-durable goods (printing and writing paper, groceries, chemicals, and periodicals), don't sell to ultimate household consumers.

Three types of operations can perform the functions of wholesale trade: wholesale distributors; manufacturers' sales branches and offices; and agents, brokers, and commission agents. As a wholesale distributor, you will probably run an independently owned and operated firm that buys and sells products of which you have taken ownership. Generally, such operations are run from one or more warehouses where inventory goods are received and later shipped to customers.

Put simply, as the owner of a wholesale distributorship, you will be buying goods to sell at a profit, much as a retailer would. The only difference is that you'll be working in a business-to-business realm by selling to retail companies and other wholesale firms like your own, and not to the buying public. This is, however, something of a traditional definition. For example, companies like Sam's Club and BJ's Warehouse have been using warehouse membership clubs, where consumers are able to buy at what appear to be wholesale prices, for some time now, thus blurring the lines. However, the traditional wholesale distributor is still a person who buys "from the source" and sells to a reseller.

Beware!
Remember that as a wholesale distributor, your customers have their own customers to satisfy. Because of this, they have more at stake than the typical consumer shopping at a discount distributor serving mainstream consumers.

Setting Up Shop

When it comes time to set up shop, your needs will vary according to what type of product you choose to specialize in. You could conceivably run a successful wholesale distribution business from your basement, but storage needs would eventually hamper the company's success. "If you're running a distribution company from home, then you're much more of a broker than a distributor," says Fein, noting that while a distributor takes title and legal ownership of the products, a broker simply facilitates the transfer of products. "However, through the use of the internet, there are some very interesting alternatives to becoming a distributor [who takes] physical possession of the product." (You can read more about using the internet in your operations in Chapter 10 of this book.)

According to Fein, wholesale distribution companies are frequently started in areas where land is not too expensive and where buying or renting warehouse space is affordable. "Generally, wholesale distributors are not located in downtown shopping areas, but off the beaten path," says Fein. "If, for example, you're serving building or electrical contractors, you'll need to choose a location in close proximity to them in order to be accessible as they go about their jobs."

What to Sell?

While brick-and-mortar sales still command a vast majority of the retail market—nearly $4.27 trillion in 2013—ecommerce sales are increasing much faster, contributing significantly to retail's overall growth in the U.S. Market research firm eMarketer estimates that U.S. retail ecommerce sales will increase 15.5 percent in 2014 to reach $304.1 billion, up from $263.3 billion in 2013. That growth will represent more than 20 percent of the total $199.4 billion increase in total retail sales for the current year.

In 2013, U.S. retail cash registers and online merchants rang up about $4.5 trillion in sales (www.emarketer.com/Article/Total-US-Retail-Sales-Top-3645-Trillion-2013-Outpace-GDP-Growth/1010756), and of that, about a quarter comes from general merchandise, apparel, and furniture sales (GAF). This is a positive for wholesale distributors, who rely heavily on retailers as customers. To measure the scope of GAF, try to imagine every consumer item sold, then remove cars, building materials, and food. The rest, including computers, clothing, sports equipment, and other items, fall into the GAF total. Such goods come directly from manufacturers or through wholesalers and brokers. Then they are sold in department, high-volume, and specialty stores—all of which will make up your client base once you open the doors of your wholesale distribution firm.

All this is good news for the startup entrepreneur looking to launch a wholesale distribution company. However, there are a few dangers that you should be aware of. For

> ⚠ **Beware!**
> Consolidation is running rampant in many industries. Before choosing your niche, do some market research on your customer base (especially if you're going to limit yourself to a particular region) to be sure those customers aren't ripe for consolidation. If they are, you could see your client base shrink quickly.

starters, consolidation is rampant in this industry, with some sectors contracting more quickly than others. For example, pharmaceutical wholesaling has consolidated more than just about any other sector, according to Fein.

To combat the consolidation trend, many independent distributors are turning to the specialty market. "Many entrepreneurs are finding success by picking up the golden crumbs that are left on the table by the national companies," Fein says. "As distribution has evolved from a local to a regional to a national business, the national companies [can't or don't want to] cost-effectively service certain types of customers. Often, small customers get left behind or are just not [profitable] for the large distributors to serve."

In addition to consolidating, the wholesale distribution industry is also evolving rapidly, which translates to both positive and negative changes. For instance, there are indications of disintermediation trends across various industries. Several years ago, strategists and futurists began predicting that companies would increasingly sell directly to consumers, cutting out distributors and any other distribution intermediaries, including some retailers. The predicted change was given a fancy term: disintermediation. It has yet to happen, but the threat persists as an increasing number of manufacturers and end users find one another directly. However, no matter what changes may be in store, smart wholesale distributors will always find a way to adapt. When companies like Amazon make their way into new industries, for example, smart distributors know how to pull out the big guns and—instead of trying to compete solely on price—deliver the knowledge, expertise, and customer service levels that keep customers coming back for more.

The Technological Edge

Today, nearly 3 billion people around the globe have access to the internet. This is good news for the wholesale distributor who is willing to be flexible in the information age. While traditional players have felt threatened by the internet as a growing sales channel, startups today will be more apt to grab technology by the horns and use it to their advantage.

As ecommerce has evolved into more than just a business opportunity, traditional "brick-and-mortar" businesses are no longer able to rely on traditional forms of selling

Bright Idea

You can take a trip on the information super-highway to visit a few of your potential competitors. Key the words "wholesale distributor" into your favorite search engine, or narrow it down geographically by adding your city and/or state to the search string.

products to their customers. Product distribution and delivery trends have been impacted as the internet has grown in popularity. Businesses must also be available to their customers via the internet. For this reason, wholesale distributors—like their vendors—can grab the opportunity to position themselves as internet-savvy firms. Using a combination of their own websites, the online resources of their manufacturers, social media sites like Facebook, Twitter, and LinkedIn, and myriad other tech tools, distributors have moved some or all of their operations into the online arena.

As with fighting the trend toward consolidation, a smart wholesaler can step up the plate and leverage a bit of ingenuity and creativity. Finding a unique niche is one sharp move, whether by serving a group of consumers that manufacturers or larger distributors can't be bothered with, or perhaps buying in bulk and then selling reduced quantities to smaller firms that don't want to make big inventory investments.

Including value-added services can also give you a competitive edge. These include, but are not limited to, simplifying the transfer of product, helping smooth out possible glitches in the information flow, and making transfer of payment easier. In other words, rather than going directly to the manufacturer—who is often more concerned with producing the hard goods than dealing with customer needs—retailers and other distributors can deal with a wholesaler who specializes in customer needs. Wholesalers can also make themselves valuable by keeping goods on hand for customers who would otherwise have to deal with long lead times when buying direct. "That availability very often makes the wholesale distributor a backup for, and extension of, the customer's own inventory system," says Fein. And ecommerce itself can be a boon to the wholesale distributor, when it comes to finding new customers and hunting down new product manufacturers and vendors to buy from.

Starting Out

For entrepreneurs looking to start their own wholesale distributorship, there are basically

Beware!

If you're planning to start a wholesale distribution business from home, check with your local zoning board about the legality of shipping and receiving merchandise at your home. For example, many cities do not allow the delivery of goods from vehicles like tractor-trailers in residential neighborhoods.

Thinking Globally

According to NAW, distributors today and in the future are faced with an unprecedented number of change drivers, as well as an accelerating pace of change. Among the more influential and persistent factors driving the change are globalization, consolidation, competition, and disintermediation. Consolidation has been reshaping distribution for at least the last 25 years, but today it is having a different effect. Previously, consolidation shifted negotiating leverage across the value chain, with larger entities typically gaining leverage (because they were able to push through price increases or demand incremental discounts) and smaller entities seeing their leverage reduced (www.naw.org/admin /files/files/FFC13bk_EXECSUM.pdf).

three avenues to choose from: buy an existing business, start from scratch or buy into a business opportunity. Buying an existing business can be costly and may even be risky, depending on the level of success and reputation of the distributorship you want to buy. The positive side of buying a business is that you can probably tap into the seller's knowledge bank, and you may even inherit his or her existing client base, which could prove extremely valuable.

The second option, starting from scratch, can also be costly, but it allows for a true "make it or break it" scenario that is guaranteed not to be preceded by an existing owner's reputation. On the downside, you will be building a reputation from scratch, which means lots of sales and marketing for at least the first two years or until your client base is large enough to reach critical mass.

The last option is perhaps the most risky, as all business opportunities must be thoroughly explored before any money or precious time is invested. However, the right opportunity can mean support, training, and quick success if the originating company has already proven itself to be profitable, reputable, and durable.

Regardless of which avenue you choose, a new distributorship will require a few key pieces of equipment to get you started. In the office, a personal computer, several phone lines, a fax machine, and access to a reliable shipping method will all be necessary. Most wholesalers drop-ship their products through the use of shipping services (UPS, DHL, FedEx, etc.), though some who deliver to their local areas use their own leased or purchased delivery vehicles. In the end, it truly depends on the product, lead times and proximity of your customer base. With the exception of the entrepreneur who is wholesaling T-shirts from his or her basement, a generous amount of warehouse space will be necessary, as will a location that is in close proximity to your customers.

During the startup process, you'll also need to assess your own financial situation and decide if you're going to start your business on a full- or part-time basis. A full-time commitment probably means quicker success, mainly because you will be devoting all your time to the new company's success.

Because the amount of startup capital necessary will be highly dependent on what you choose to sell, the numbers vary. For instance, an Ohio-based wholesale distributor of men's ties and belts, Keith Schwartz (now president at Nicole Brayden Gifts and Divinity Boutique in Ohio), started On Target Promotions with $700 worth of closeout ties, bought from a manufacturer, and a few basic pieces of office equipment. At the higher end of the spectrum, a Virginia-based distributor of fine wines started with $1.5 million used mainly for inventory, a large warehouse, internal necessities (pallet racking, pallets, forklift), and a few Chevrolet Astro vans for delivery.

Like most startups, the average wholesale distributor will need to be in business two to five years to be profitable. There are exceptions, of course. Take, for example, the ambitious entrepreneur who sets up his garage as a warehouse to stock small hand tools. Using his own vehicle and relying on the low overhead that his home provides, he could conceivably start making money within 6 to 12 months.

"Wholesale distribution is a very large segment of the economy and constitutes about 5.6 percent of the nation's GDP," says Pembroke Consulting Inc.'s Fein. "That said, there are many different subsegments and industries within the realm of wholesale distribution, and some offer much greater opportunities than others."

Among those subsegments are wholesale distributors who specialize in a unique niche (e.g., the distributor who sells specialty foods to grocery stores); larger distributors who sell everything from soup to nuts (e.g., the distributor with warehouses nationwide and a large stock of various, unrelated closeout items); and midsized distributors who choose an industry (e.g., hand tools) and offer a variety of products to myriad customers.

Regardless of which subsegment you choose, this book will give you the information you need to get started. In the next chapter, we'll examine the operational aspect of owning a wholesale distribution business.

Dollar Stretcher

To avoid spending excess money during the start-up phase, list everything you think you need and then ask yourself: Why do I need this item? How will it help me be more productive? Can I do without it for six months or a year while my business is getting started? Do this for every purchase, and you'll avoid the urge to spend on nonessential items.

Growth of the
Wholesale Distribution Sector

According to the National Association of Wholesaler-Distributors (NAW), the nation's real gross domestic product (GDP) grew 2.7 percent in 2013 and U.S. Industrial Production (NAW's benchmark for the overall economy) rose 2.6 percent during the same period. "Overall, it was a growth year for the U.S. economy, on target with what we told NAW Direct Members last year," write NAW Senior Economic Advisor Alan Beaulieu and Economist Jon Murphy.

The Wholesale Trade Industry itself accounts for about 5.6 percent of the overall economy, the NAW reports, and wholesaler-distributors are a crucial part of the supply chain in other larger sectors of the economy such as manufacturing, retail trade, and healthcare—meaning that wholesale trade's contributions to the overall economy are much larger than the 5.6 percent figure would indicate.

According to NAW, total wholesale trade for the most recent 12 months as of the first quarter of 2013 was up 4.2 percent from 2012, totaling $5.13 trillion. Nearly all segments of wholesale trade were up on the year, according to NAW, with the exceptions of metals and minerals and sporting goods, games, toys, and jewelry. At the time, NAW was detecting weakness developing in raw farm products—a condition that was likely to persist in the first half of 2014. Durable goods ended the year up 4.4 percent, NAW reports, and nondurable goods grew 4.1 percent.

A growing labor market helped support U.S. economic growth in 2013, and the wholesale distribution industry did its part. Wholesale trade employment averaged 5.8 million workers in 2013, a 1.6 percent gain from 2012, according to NAW. (The economy as a whole added jobs at a 1.0 percent clip.) "Wholesale trade employment rising at a faster pace than the overall economy suggests the industry is improving," said Beaulieu and Murphy.

Frantz Group reports that for the period between 2010 and 2015, the output of the U.S. wholesale distribution industry was forecast to grow at an annual compounded rate of 6 percent. The group is bullish on future opportunities for wholesale distributors, noting that over the last 10 years, while distributor revenue grew nearly 50 percent—with computers, electrical goods, and machinery leading the pack—retailers showed 40 percent growth, and the U.S. economy saw 30 percent growth.

"Considering that the decade in question included the 'ugliest financial disaster since the Great Depression,'" the Frantz Group reports, "and that the U.S. economy still managed to show 30 percent growth on average, we'd say 'above average' works well enough."

Operations

ow that you have the "big picture" view of

the wholesale distribution business, and now that you know your

potential for success as a startup business owner, we'll give you

the lowdown on just how your new company will operate.

A wholesale distributor's initial steps when ven-

turing into the entrepreneurial landscape include defining a customer base and locating reliable sources of product. The latter will soon become commonly known as your "vendors" or "suppliers."

There are, of course, myriad other startup considerations that we'll discuss in this book. The cornerstone of every distribution cycle, however, is the basic flow of product from manufacturer to distributor to customer. As a wholesale distributor, your position on that supply chain (a supply chain is a set of resources and processes that begins with the sourcing of raw material and extends through the delivery of items to the final consumer) will involve matching up the manufacturer and customer by obtaining quality products at a reasonable price and then selling them to the companies that need them.

In its simplest form, distribution means purchasing a product from a source—usually a manufacturer, but sometimes another distributor—and selling it to your customer. As a wholesale distributor, you will specialize in selling to customers—and even other distributors—who are in the business of selling to end users (usually the general public). It's one of the purest examples of the business-to-business function, as opposed to a business-to-consumer function, in which companies sell to the general public.

Weighing It Out: Operating Costs

No two distribution companies are alike, and each has its own unique needs. The entrepreneur who is selling closeout T-shirts from his basement, for example, has very different startup financial needs than the one selling power tools from a warehouse in the middle of an industrial park.

Regardless of where a distributor sets up shop (read more about where to establish your company in Chapter 6 of this book), some basic operating costs apply across the board. For starters, necessities such as office space, a telephone, fax machine, and personal computer will make up the core of your business. (Read more about specialized equipment necessary for wholesale distributors in Chapter 7.) This means an office rental fee if you're working from anywhere but home, a telephone bill and internet access fees. (Find out more about standard office equipment in Chapter 7 of this book.)

No matter what type of products you plan to carry, you'll need some type of warehouse or storage space in which to store them; this means a leasing fee. Remember that if you lease a

Dollar Stretcher

Even if you absolutely need to lease warehouse space, remember that you can still handle operations from a homebased office. Not only will this allow for 24-hour access to your nascent firm (sometimes a necessity in the "getting started" phase of business), but it will also allow you to write off a portion of your home for tax purposes.

The Distributor's Daily Checklist

Without a daily agenda, who knows if you're actually completing all the tasks that need to be done? Try using the following checklist as a guide when going through your daily activities:

❑ Check phone messages, incoming faxes, and email messages from the night before (especially if you're dealing with customers in other states or countries; they may have quitting times that are later than yours).

❑ If any of those messages were product orders, confirm them with the customers (if necessary) and place the orders with the appropriate vendors.

❑ Review the day's delivery and/or shipping schedule. If you're delivering to a local area, be sure to call all nearby customers to see if they need anything while you're in the area.

❑ Set up a sales call contact sheet (see page 16 for an example) and set a reasonable goal for how many new customers your efforts should net each week.

❑ Follow up with vendors on any deliveries you're expecting or any that may be overdue.

❑ Handle any internal functions that may need attention: hiring or firing employees, accounting and bookkeeping, financial projections, etc.

❑ Arrange for any late-day shipments (if applicable) to customers who may have called in for emergency deliveries.

❑ Prepare a delivery schedule for the following day.

warehouse that has room for office space, you can combine both on one bill. If you're delivering locally, you'll also need an adequate vehicle to get around in. If your customer base is located further than 50 miles from your home base, then you'll also need to set up a working relationship with one or more shipping companies like UPS, FedEx, or the U.S. Postal Service. Most distributors serve a mixed client base; some of the merchandise you move can be delivered via truck, while some will require shipping services. (Read more about whether you should lease or buy your vehicles in Chapter 7.)

While they may sound a bit overwhelming, the above necessities don't always have to be expensive—especially not during the startup phase. For example, Keith Schwartz, owner of numerous wholesale distribution businesses, started his wholesale tie and belt distributorship from the corner of his living room. With no equipment other than a phone, fax machine, and computer, he grew his company from the living

▲

Beware!

Distributors can fall into the rut of offering customers only products that they've already purchased. Don't let this happen to you. Instead, make customers special offers, tell them about new product offerings, and introduce them to products they may have never thought of. A little customer education goes a long way, so keep them informed!

room to the basement to the garage and then into a shared warehouse space (the entire process took five years).

To avoid liability early on in his entrepreneurial venture, Schwartz rented pallet space in someone else's warehouse, where he stored his closeout ties and belts. This meant lower overhead for the entrepreneur, along with no utility bills, leases, or costly insurance policies in his name. In fact, it wasn't until he penned a deal with a Michigan distributor for a large project that he had to store product and re-label the closeout ties with his firm's own insignia. As a result, he finally rented a 1,000-square-foot warehouse space. But even that was shared, this time with another Ohio distributor. "I don't believe in having any liability if I don't have to have it," he says. "A warehouse is a liability."

Whether you choose to store product in your hall closet or in a 10,000-square-foot warehouse is highly dependent on your budget and on the size of the products you're distributing. Either way, this book will help you figure out what will work best.

The Day-to-Day Routine

Like many other businesses, wholesale distributors perform sales and marketing, accounting, shipping and receiving, and customer service functions on a daily basis. They also handle tasks like contacting existing and prospective customers, processing orders, supporting customers who need help with problems that may crop up, and doing market research (for example, who better than the "in the trenches" distributor to find out if a manufacturer's new product will be viable in a particular market?).

"One reason that wholesale distributors have increased their share of total wholesale sales is that they can perform these functions more effectively and efficiently than manufacturers or customers," comments Adam Fein of Philadelphia-based Pembroke Consulting Inc.

Tip...

Smart Tip

Even though your business is just starting up, you should avoid the Rolodex and use a computer-based database system to track clients and business partners. You'll want to do this eventually anyway, so get in the habit of using the electronic version now, and you'll be ahead of the game.

To handle all these tasks and whatever else may come their way during the course of the day, most distributors rely on specialized software packages that tackle such functions as inventory control, shipping and receiving, accounting, client management, and barcoding (the application of computerized UPC codes to track inventory).

And while not every distributor has adopted the high-tech way of doing business, those who have are reaping the rewards of their investments. . Los Angeles, California-based yoga and fitness distributor and training studio YogaFit Inc., for example, has been slowly tweaking its automation strategy over the past few years, according to Beth Shaw, founder and president. Shaw says the 15-employee company sells through a website that tracks orders and manages inventory, and the company also makes use of networking among its various computers and a database management program to maintain and update client information. In business since 1994, Shaw says technology has helped increase her productivity while cutting down on the amount of time spent on repetitive activities, such as entering addresses used to create mailing labels for catalogs and individual orders. Adds Shaw, "It's imperative that any new distributor realize from day one that technology will make their lives much, much easier."

Tracking Your Efforts

There's no room for complacency in business, and the wholesale distributor who contacts both existing and potential customers on a regular basis gains an edge over competitors who may not be so diligent. Sometimes you may even get a sale just by being there at the right time. In other words, the customer on the other end of the phone would have bought those 12 cases of masking tape from another distributor if you hadn't called at the right moment and told him you'd be in his area the next morning.

To keep track of whom you call, what you offer them, and when you should call again, use a call log. This can be done via a contact management database like ACT!, Sugar, or even Microsoft Outlook. Another option is to do it the old-fashioned way (which might be necessary at first) and just keep a written log using multiple sales call contact sheets (see page 16 for a form you can use).

As your customer base grows, you may need to add more categories to your sales call contact sheet. Be flexible, and remember to always make extra offers to your customers. It may be weeks before they decide to take you up on the offer, but your customers will always appreciate your willingness to introduce them to new products.

Sales Call Contact Sheet

Customer name: _____

Company name: _____

Address: _____

Phone number: _____

Products frequently purchased: _____

Possible cross-sells and upsells: _____

CALLS

Date: _____

Time: _____

Contact's name: _____

Purchases: _____

Delivery date: _____

Additional products offered: _____

_____

Notes: _____

_____

_____

_____

_____

Staying on Top of an Evolving Industry

With threats of direct selling (when the manufacturer sells to the end user or other customer instead of using a distributor), web-only distributors, industry consolidation and disintermediation (the elimination of the middleman in the sales process) threatening their industry, distributors appear to be facing an uncertain future. However, there will always be a need for the entrepreneur who can provide services and support that a manufacturer simply doesn't have the time or resources to offer.

Bright Idea

When pitching your offerings to new customers, bring along comparison figures that show how much they can save by buying from you in smaller, more digestible quantities. For example, you might let them know that you're passing on a 5 percent discount to them thanks to your ability to buy in larger quantities at wholesale prices.

In other words, successful distributors in today's rapidly evolving business landscape will be those who think beyond the product to other value-added services they can provide. For example, a small grocery store may sell only 20 flashlights annually. In such a situation, buying direct from the manufacturer would hardly be feasible, since most manufacturers sell in large quantities (known as "lots"). That's where the distributor comes in. By purchasing 2,000 of the flashlights and then selling them to their customers (in this case, retailers who sell to the general public), the distributor is fulfilling a true need. Not only is the customer able to save money by purchasing from someone who bought an entire lot of the product, but they can avoid stocking 2,000 flashlights on their shelves for an inordinate amount of time.

And while customers obviously benefit from the distributor's ability to divide large quantities, manufacturers also benefit. The size of a wholesale distributor's purchase serves a valuable function by satisfying the manufacturer's need for efficiency because they can manufacture and ship in large quantities as opposed to smaller lots. It's a true win-win-win situation for all three parties, and it's one all wholesale distributors should work to maximize as they progress in business.

In the next chapter, we'll discuss how to stay ahead of the curve by researching your market, defining who your customers are, and concentrating on those who will bring your company the most profits.

Defining and Researching Your Market

Because every company relies on a pool of customers to sell its products and/or services to, the next logical step in the startup process involves defining exactly who will be included in that pool. Defining this group early on will allow you to develop business strategies, define your mission or answer the question "why am I in business?" and tailor your operations to meet the needs of your customer base.

As a wholesale distributor, your choice of customers includes:

Smart Tip

Before bidding on a government project, read the fine print on the request for proposal (RFP). Often, government orders require special packaging and shipping that can inflate your costs for processing and shipping the order.

- *Retail businesses.* This includes establishments like grocery stores, independent retail stores, large department stores, and power retailers like Walmart and Target.

- *Retail distributors.* This includes the distributors who sell to those retailers that you may find impenetrable on your own. For example, if you can't "get in" at a power retailer like Walmart, you may be able to sell to one of its distributors.

- *Exporters.* These are companies that collect U.S.-manufactured goods and ship them overseas.

- *Other wholesale distributors.* It's always best to buy from the source, but that isn't always possible, due to exclusive contracts and issues like one-time needs (e.g., a distributor who needs ten hard hats for a customer who is particular about buying one brand). For this reason, wholesale distributors often find themselves selling to other distributors.

- *The federal government.* Uncle Sam is always looking for items that wholesale distributors sell. In fact, for wholesale distributors, selling to the government presents a great opportunity. For the most part, it's a matter of filling out the appropriate forms and getting on a "bid list." After you become an official government supplier, the various buying agencies will either fax or email you requests for bids for materials needed by schools, various agencies, shipyards, and other facilities.

For a small wholesale distributor, there are some great advantages to selling to the government, but the process can also be challenging in that such orders often require a lengthy bidding process before any contracts are awarded. Since opening her Los Angeles, California, distributorship in 1994, Beth Shaw of YogaFit Inc. says she's made several successful sales to the government. Currently, the firm sells its exercise education programs and several styles of yoga mats to Army bases and other entities. In fact, she says YogaFit is the only such company that's approved by the GI Bill and says the firm recently developed a 100-hour YogaFit Warriors certification program that focuses on military-related conditions like post traumatic stress disorder (PTSD), among other issues. Calling government sales "a good avenue" for wholesale distributors, Shaw says it's also one that's often overlooked, "especially by small businesses."

Bright Idea

If you're afraid that your market research surveys will be ignored or delayed, try offering a perk that will motivate your recipients to share their views with you. For example, you might try offering 10 percent off of the recipient's first purchase in exchange for returning the survey by a certain date.

Market Research Tactics

To reach customers other than the government (which tends to act as a captive audience that you can deal with on a separate basis from the rest of your customer pool), you will first need to do some basic market research. Done properly, this will aid in the establishment of your wholesale distribution business and will help you be better prepared before opening the doors to your company.

Market research for a business can run from a simple series of phone calls to very expensive and complex studies. Unfortunately, too many small businesses—wholesale distributors included—do little or no market research and end up missing out on valuable information concerning their customers' wants and needs. It's this information that cannot only increase sales but also help you avoid making major mistakes during the early stages of business.

One of the cornerstones of market research is determining customer needs in the marketplace. This research is conducted with both current (if applicable) and targeted customers. Using a well-thought-out market research plan, you can uncover what is driving your customers' companies, what their needs are, and what features they're seeking in the products and services you plan to offer. This information will also help you determine the market potential for a product or service, including what kind of demand already exists for the product and what price customers are willing to pay.

Once your company is established, you will also want to do market research that assesses current customer satisfaction. Wholesale distributors must stay abreast of issues such as whether they are serving their current customers well. Through effective market research, problems can be corrected, new products or services can be developed, and a closer relationship fostered with existing customers.

Online Surveys

With 3 billion potential consumers worldwide currently using the internet and a higher percentage of them based in North America, why not take advantage of this huge consumer base by conducting online market research surveys?

For the wholesale distributor, online surveys can be a true godsend. They are relatively inexpensive to produce. They are also fast, targeted, innovative, and accurate.

Currently, there are several online services that offer business owners a way to produce and analyze such surveys (for example, SurveyMonkey and FluidSurveys). Most offer do-it-yourself options, which are handy for firms that have a viable list of recipients and extra hands to do the tabulating. At FluidSurvey.com, for example, you can sign up for free and get unlimited surveys, 20 questions/survey, 150 responses/survey, and real-time response analysis. The pro version costs $17 a month and includes a longer list of services. To get started, simply key the words "online surveys" into your favorite search engine. From there, pick a few companies, ask for and check references, and then do a test run based on your needs. You may be surprised at how fast and efficient it is to do market research online.

Key Considerations

Before starting her market basket importing and distributing firm in 2008, Laura Benson, owner and founder of Minneapolis, Minnesota.-based Jeanne Beatrice, LLC, did extensive research into the potential market for her unique products. She credits her legal career with helping out during this due diligence phase. "I was online constantly, just seeing what else was being sold out there, where the products were coming from, and just educating myself on my new potential venture," says Benson. "At the time, I didn't know where specific styles were produced; today you can show me a random basket and I'll be able to tell you exactly what country it came from. Early on I didn't know that."

During the market research phase, Benson says she came upon just one other U.S. company that was selling the beautiful, European baskets that she was looking to import and sell to her own customers. And while the baskets that her competitor was selling were from Morocco (where Benson's also hail from) she says she didn't readily identify that company as a threat. Other companies have come and gone over the last eight years, she adds, "but they usually disappear pretty quickly because this isn't an easy business to be in."

According to Adam Fein of Philadelphia-based Pembroke Consulting Inc., new wholesale distribution businesses have two general issues to consider during the market research phase:

1. Will the industry channel continue to be viable? According to Fein, the internet

Dollar Stretcher

If your startup budget doesn't allow for the hiring of a market research firm and your time is too limited to do the market research on your own, try tapping into one or more of the publications, associations, and professional organizations listed in the Appendix of this book. Some organizations compile and distribute industry-specific market research data to their members, often at no cost.

has restructured many distribution channels. Those thinking of starting a wholesale distribution business should first ensure that their company will actually provide high value to their customers. This is necessary because wholesale distributors are finding themselves being disintermediated, or cut out of the channel, by manufacturers who choose to sell directly to customers and customers who choose to buy directly from manufacturers.

2. What competitors are currently in the market? Some distribution industries are very fragmented, meaning that they're made up of thousands of small, privately-held companies. According to Fein, such companies tend to come and go because the challenges posed to new companies opening up in the industry. On the other hand, some distribution industries have become highly consolidated and are dominated by large, national corporations. As a result, he says, in consolidated industries there are fewer opportunities for a general-service, broad-based wholesale distribution company but many opportunities for the niche or specialized distributor.

Getting to Know You

Before trying to figure out just what will make potential customers open their wallets and start buying from your new wholesale distributorship, ask them the following questions:

○ How often do you buy products from wholesale distributors?

○ What are the three products you purchase most often from wholesale distributors?

○ If a new wholesale distributor of (fill in the blank with your offerings) in (your city and state) were to open, would you consider using it as a new source of products?

○ How satisfied are you with the service you're currently getting from your distributor of (fill in the blank with your offerings)?

○ What is the number one thing you expect from a distributor?

○ Do you feel you're currently getting that from your distributor of (fill in the blank with your offerings)?

○ What are the top three things you'd like to see from a new distributor?

▲

> **Beware!**
> Some online survey companies continually screen the same group of candidates. Before working with a survey company, be sure to inquire about its recipient list, how the recipients are gathered and screened, and what the recipients' specific demographics are.

Check Out the Competition

As Fein points out, researching the competition is crucial. You'll want to take a regional, national, and international (if applicable) view of what is going on around you in distribution circles. If you're planning to offer products to a regional group of potential buyers, be sure that there isn't already a niche player in your area. You can find out whether there is by calling the buyers themselves (those who are purchasing product for retail stores, for example), and asking them from whom they are buying. Because most buyers are out to get the best possible deal and are eager to work with quality suppliers, most will gladly share this information with you.

Doing a bit of competitive intelligence (i.e., getting the lowdown on the competition) before you open your doors will go a long way. Here are a few "talking points" to discuss with distributors who are already in your market. (We're not saying all of them will give up the information in detail, but it's worth a shot!)

- What products and services does your company specialize in?
- How is the local market (or the national or international market, depending on your scope) in terms of customer loyalty and its willingness to try new sources of product and new products in general?
- What is the average markup of your products?
- Do you find that this markup is acceptable to customers, or do you find yourself negotiating on a regular basis?
- How long did it take for your company to become profitable? Were there any unusual variables that came into play

> **Dollar Stretcher**
> The internet is a great, cheap place where small businesses can gain competitive intelligence. Check out your industry's trade magazines and associations and then go to a press release site like PR Newswire, PR Web, Marketwire, and openPR to see what information your competitors are sharing with the rest of the world. Also check out social networking platforms like Facebook, Twitter, and LinkedIn—all of which can provide a plethora of information, customer feedback, and other tidbits about companies in your industry.

(e.g., was the company spun off from an already successful firm, thus leading to a quicker payoff)?

- Overall, what are your thoughts on a new business coming into the market to sell (fill in the blank with your products)?

Finding a Profitable Niche

Once you have done the necessary research on your soon-to-be customers and competitors, you will have a much better idea what type of niche your new company can fill. Profitable niches in today's wholesale distribution arena include, but are certainly not limited to, reselling products that require some degree of education on the seller's part. Take, for example, the pencil analogy: Selling traditional pencils is easy, but selling mechanical pencils that require a specific technique—and a refill—takes smarts. In the latter situation, a wholesale distributor comes in extremely handy because they can educate the customer, who can then educate his own end user, about the benefits and operations of the mechanical pencil.

In other words, what matters is not so much what you sell, but how you sell it. There are profitable opportunities in every industry—from beauty supplies to hand tools, beverages to snack foods. No matter what they're selling, wholesale distributors are discovering ways to reaffirm their value to suppliers and customers by revealing the superior service they have to offer, as well as the cost-saving efficiencies created by those services. This mindset opens up a wealth of opportunities to provide greater attention to the individual needs of customers, a chance to develop margin growth, and greater flexibility in product offerings and diversification of the business.

Smart Tip

You might choose to distribute products to a particular region, but you'll probably be propositioned by far-flung companies to ship product outside your area (especially with the growth of the internet, which can make a company website available to the world with just a few keystrokes). Develop a company-wide plan for handling these types of situations.

Beware!

Distributors who put too many eggs in one basket by catering only to a select group of customers may find themselves empty-handed when their customer base suffers an economic downturn. For example, the agriculture industry recently had a particularly bad year, so distributors of tools used to make farming equipment were adversely affected. Be smart and keep an eye open for new places to sell product and for economic trends that might affect your company down the road.

Remember—it wasn't too long ago that many people thought corporate behemoths like Sears and Home Depot would be the demise of the small contractor and the wholesale distributor, respectively. Yet to this day, they have not had a significant impact on either (although online, price-competitive sites like Amazon are currently making a mark in various industries and are definitely worth paying attention to.)

The whole trick, of course, is to find that niche and make it work for you. In wholesale distribution, a niche is a particular area where your company can most excel and prosper—be it selling tie-dyed T-shirts, roller bearings, or sneakers. While some entrepreneurs may find their niche in a diverse area (for example, closeout goods purchased from manufacturers), others may wish to specialize (unique barstools that will be sold to regional bars and pubs).

On the other side of the coin, too much product and geographical specialization can hamper success. Take the barstool example. Let's say you were going to go with this idea but that in six months you'd already sold as many barstools as you could to the customer base within a 40-mile radius of your location. At that point, you would want to diversify your offerings, perhaps adding other bar-related items like dartboards, pool cues, and other types of chairs.

The decision is yours: You can go into the wholesale distribution arena with a full menu of goods or a limited selection. Usually that decision will be based on your finances, the amount of time you'll be able to devote to the business, and the resources available to you. Regardless of the choices you make, remember that market research provides critical information that enables a business to successfully go to market, and wholesale distributors should do as much as they can—on an ongoing basis. It is better to do simple research routinely than to shell out a lot of money once on a big research information project that may quickly become outdated.

In the next chapter, we'll discuss several issues you'll have to consider before opening your doors, including choosing a business name, what types of business licenses are required, and the various professional services you may need during the startup phase and beyond.

4

Structuring
Your Business

You've defined your market and determined
the viability of your business idea. Now get ready to focus on a
few important ingredients that go into running a successful
business. Some issues will be decided at the outset and pretty
much forgotten about while you concentrate on getting your
company profitable (issues like business structure, company

name and the necessary licenses). Other matters are constantly evolving (for example, business insurance and the use of outside professionals, both of which will change as your business grows). Read on for more information about structuring your wholesale distributorship to achieve maximum success.

Choosing a Name that Fits

The world is littered with business names. Some leave an impression, others do not, and still others leave people wondering "What the heck does that company do?" Take a look at your competitors to find out what type of name will best fit your business. Because your goal is not to attract the mainstream public, you'll want to come up with a catchy moniker that befits a true business-to-business operation.

For a wholesale distribution firm, consider descriptive names that express exactly what their firm does. While names like "Kraft" and "Dell" may work well for large firms that possess big advertising and branding budgets, the name "City Office Supply" would probably work well for a small office equipment distributor. Esoteric names may sound nice, but it's more beneficial if your customers can tell what you do by simply looking at your business card, sign or advertisement.

Beth Shaw of Los Angeles, California-based YogaFit Inc. says her company name does just that and that it came to her during a bicycle ride in the early 1990s. She says she wanted a name that described what her firm did and that YogaFit just, well, fit. "I wanted it to be very clear to my customers," says Shaw. "So far, so good."

Distributors often rely on their primary product line, supplier, or geographical location to dictate their company's names. For example, one successful Maryland-based distributor of safety supplies uses "Safeware Inc.," while a distributor in Massachusetts that specializes in fasteners has found success with "Atlantic Fasteners." Still others rely on the family names of their founders to help them cut through the clutter. "Orco Supply," a California-based building supply distributor, and "B.C. MacDonald," a cutting tool distributor in Missouri, have both found success with this strategy.

Keith Schwartz of the Warrensville Heights, Ohio-based wholesale accessories distributorship says his firm's name has changed multiple times since its inception. "Each time, we changed it based on what we were trying to accomplish in the sales department and what image we needed to portray to our customers," he explains. "Our market concept is to develop a wide assortment

> **Tip...**
>
> **Smart Tip**
> Make sure your company name clearly defines your business for several years into the future. Changing a company name—should you choose to diversify into a different business area in a few years—can be a costly, time-intensive proposition.

of seasonal promotions that can be sold to the same customers. This gives us a reason to visit our customers every month and gives them a stronger reason to buy from us."

Regardless of what route you take when naming your business—naming it after yourself, getting help from a marketing guru, or sticking with something that relates to your line of business—the key is to come up with something that will stick in your customers' minds as your wholesale distribution company grows, expands and prospers.

On a Mission:
Developing a Positioning Statement

Some business owners keep them in their heads, others write them down on scraps of paper, and still others put them in formal documents like business plans. Put simply, a company mission statement tells the world exactly why you're in business. As your company grows, such statements of purpose circulate throughout the organization so that your employees can develop strategies that support your overall mission and vision. It also helps clearly state the major way you differentiate the company and provide unique benefits to customers.

A mission statement should focus on the very reasons that your firm is in business: to create opportunities and to serve the needs of your customers. Write your own mission statement around these two elements, and in that order. Remember that while your main mission is to serve your customer base with quality products in a timely, efficient fashion, you must also factor in the "opportunity" aspect of the mission or risk becoming a dissatisfied business owner. A distributor who sells surplus inventory to discount retailers, for example, would do well by creating a mission statement surrounding not only its business purpose, but also the key opportunities (both for employees and the business owner) that the company can tap during the course of business. A wholesale distributor who specializes in safety-related equipment for industrial customers can take a similar tack but with a tighter focus on how its products and services can help reduce on-the-job injuries and even deaths.

Beware!
Don't let your mission statement corner you into doing business in an unprofitable manner. As your distributorship grows, remember that it may need to be tweaked to meet changing market demands, evolving customer needs, and new opportunities. Sticking to your core values is always recommended, but don't let your mission statement make you miss out on a great opportunity.

▲

Riding the Trends

Talk about being in the right place at the right time. Back in 1994, Beth Shaw couldn't have possibly predicted the booming yoga trend that would take hold just a few years after founding her firm. Still, this budding entrepreneur saw opportunity in distributing yoga and exercise equipment, clothing, and accessories. Today, Los Angeles, California-based YogaFit has 15 full-time employees and about 75 independent contractors/salespeople who sell products nationwide. A website complements their efforts and helps the firm reach out to customers in diverse geographic areas. The combined efforts have pushed the company to success over the last few years—right along with the national yoga and exercise trend, which shows no sign of letting up anytime soon. Shaw, who stays on top of trends by reading industry magazines and paying attention to the sheer number of Americans who practice yoga and fitness, says, "Business has really boomed over the last ten years." She sees no end in sight and credits her own early insights with helping her wholesale distributorship achieve success.

Perhaps the easiest way for a new distributorship to define its purpose is to drill down to its core business: buying from manufacturers and other sources and selling to a defined customer base. From there, get introspective and decide what you'd like your company to be known for and how you can best convey these goals in a simple statement.

Business Structure

There are several choices of business structure for the wholesale distributor, though most business owners choose to incorporate through either an S corporation or LLC (limited liability company) status. Protection from liability and tax savings are the two primary reasons small businesses incorporate, with many starting out as a sole proprietorship and later switching to an incorporated structure when the business grows to the point where it's warranted.

YogaFit's Shaw says she incorporated her company in 1997 after three years of running it as a sole proprietorship. She chose the C corporation route and says that while it has helped "legitimize" her company, it has also created more paperwork and taxation (since C corporation revenues are taxed on a company and personal basis). "Ultimately, I think every distributor has to incorporate," says Shaw. "When your company grows to a certain point, it's something that should be done."

Smart Tip

Tip...

Because business incorporation offers the best form of protection for the wholesale distributor, it is the ideal structure for new entrepreneurs in this field. However, the wholesale distributor who, in the interest of time and money, chooses to get established as a sole proprietorship first can certainly incorporate in the future, once his or her company is up and running.

According to Adam Fein of Philadelphia-based Pembroke Consulting Inc., many wholesale distributors with loyal, stable customer bases eventually end up being passed on from one generation to the next. "Many distributors today are second-, third-, and even fourth-generation entrepreneurs," he says. "And many wholesale distributors are mom-and-pop operations that tend to have many family members on the payroll."

When considering legal structures, it is wise for the new distributor to consider the fact that his or her business may last for multiple decades; this makes planning very important. A partnership formed with a nonfamily member that dissolves upon one partner's death may leave heirs an estate but may leave the entrepreneur who wanted to carry on the business out in the cold.

Help! I Need Somebody!

When Keith Schwartz started a wholesale distribution business selling men's belts and ties, he knew he wanted to incorporate it right away. Unfortunately, his financial situation didn't allow for the hiring of a lawyer to do the incorporation and an accountant to keep his books. The solution? He enlisted his accountant father to help him out.

"Those first few years were a real struggle," says Schwartz. "I credit my success to my father, who is an accountant and who handled my company's accounting and taxes those first couple years."

Because of his father's help, Schwartz estimates he saved about $5,000 annually. "That extra money, paid to someone to do tax returns, would have put me out of business during my first few years," he says, adding that Ohio, as well as various other states, distributes a helpful small-business packet that he utilized during his startup. "As soon as you incorporate your company, there are so many tax issues that it can be a real nightmare if you don't know what you're doing."

The Right Amount of Insurance

Wholesale distributors generally must carry the same amount and types of insurance that the typical company needs. This includes property and contents insurance, fire insurance, business interruption insurance, and other necessities that your insurance agent can discuss with you.

Don Mikovch, president of Alexandria, Virginia-based Borvin Beverage, a wholesale wine distributor, says his firm is always "looking for and inquiring about insurance." He adds that in addition to normal business coverage, a few of his larger retail customers like Sam's Club and Wal-Mart require an additional $2 million worth of business insurance. "This covers those retailers up to a certain dollar amount just in case one of our delivery people is on their property and has an accident," he says.

Dollar Stretcher

Before choosing a professional via a random online search, take a look at your own circle of friends and family. Is there a lawyer who can help you incorporate? Or perhaps an accountant who will show you the ropes of corporate income taxes? Tapping into their knowledge banks can be beneficial during your business's early stages.

Obtaining the Right Licenses

Dollar Stretcher

There are various websites that provide multiple insurance quotes with a few simple keystrokes. Check out any of these sites for more information: NetQuote (www.net quote.com), eInsurance (www.einsurance.com), or Commercial Insurance (www.commercial insurance.net).

Much like the insurance issue, licenses for new wholesale distributors are a fairly straightforward matter. You'll need an occupational license, and a license to collect sales and use tax, if applicable. (For more information on sales tax, see Chapter 11 of this book.) Licensure requirements vary by state, so check with your state and local governments to obtain all the information you'll need to get started.

In addition to business licenses, distributors may consider becoming ISO 9001 quality management certified. This designation is the standard for quality documentation in business. Put simply, it's a quality standard that can be used by corporations throughout the global community as a trademark for verifying the quality of services and product provided by a given distribution company. For example, a manufacturer in Korea who is ISO 9001-certified is working on the same quality standards as your ISO 9001-certified wholesale distribution firm in Boise, Idaho. So what's the importance of this certification for distributors? Basically, peace of mind and a knowledge that the products you're selling to customers will uphold your own standards and that they won't disappoint your customers. (Learn from about ISO certification online at: www.iso.org.)

Professionals at Your Service

No man is an island, and neither is the aspiring entrepreneur. We all need help at some time or another, and professionals like lawyers, accountants, and insurance agents can serve a valuable purpose throughout the life of your company. Other professionals such as marketing gurus and business consultants can also come in handy. For example, if your wholesale distribution business is going to have a store area, you'll want to enlist the knowledge of someone who has experience in merchandising.

Such professionals come at a price, of course, so shop around. For instance, if you need an accountant or financial consultant to help you determine the best way to incorporate your company, then be sure to do your homework ahead of time. Know what paperwork and numbers need to be in order before approaching a professional for help.

Other professionals who may come in handy for a wholesale distributor on an independent consulting basis are experienced salespeople and purchasing professionals. If you can find one who is retired or who will work for you on a short-term basis, you'll be able to learn a lot about sourcing, negotiating, selling and pricing from such professionals.

Ask other professionals in your community to recommend the names of good business attorneys or accountants.

Once you've decided on your business name and structure, and after investigating your city and state laws regarding business licenses, you'll be ready to start thinking about how you're going to finance your new entity. In the next chapter, we will take a look at financing your wholesale distribution business, including how much money you'll need to begin, how long it will take to get profitable, and what methods other distributors have used to get started.

Bright Idea

Once your wholesale distribution business is up and running, you may want to become ISO 9001-certified. Learn more about the process and what it's all about in "ISO Standards Translated Into Plain English" at http://praxiom.com. Also, check out the International Organization for Standardization at www.iso. ch/iso/en/ISO Online.frontpage, which contains various links and other information related to ISO 9000 certification.

Raising
Money

Ask any wholesale distributor what his or her biggest challenge was during the startup phase and the answer is likely to be "raising money." It's a common gripe for small-business owners, who often have to get super creative when trying to get startup capital, but one that can be overcome by determined entrepreneurs who believe in their dreams.

Pinpointing a Startup Number

While entrepreneurs in some industries seem to be able to raise money with a snap of their fingers, most have to take a more detailed approach to the process. Perhaps the best starting point is to figure out just how much you need.

In the wholesale distribution sector, startup numbers vary widely, depending on what type of company you're starting, how much inventory will be necessary, and what type of delivery systems you'll be using. For example, Keith Schwartz, who got his start selling belts and ties from his basement in Warrensville Heights, Ohio, started On Target Promotions with $700, while Don Mikovch, president of the wine distributor Borvin Beverage in Alexandria, Virginia, required $1.5 million. While Schwartz worked from a desk and only needed a small area in which to store his goods, Mikovch required a large amount of specialized storage space for his wines—and a safe method of transporting the bottles to his retailers.

The basic equipment needed for your wholesale distributorship will be highly dependent on what you choose to sell. If you plan to stock heavy items, then you should invest in a forklift (some run on fuel or propane, others are man-powered) to save yourself some strain. Pallets are useful for stocking and pallet racking is used to store the pallets and keep them in order for inventory purposes.

For distributors who are sourcing, storing, and selling bulky goods (such as floor tile, for example), a warehouse of sufficient size, based on the size of products you're selling and the amount of inventory you'll be stocking, is a necessity. (You can read more about leasing warehouse space in Chapter 6 of this book.) To ensure that the distribution process operates smoothly, select a location that allows you to move around efficiently and that includes the necessary storage equipment (such as pallet racking, on which you can store pallets). Don't forget to leave room for a forklift to be able to maneuver between racks of pallets and shelves stored in the warehouse.

As a startup distributor, your initial inventory investment will depend on what you're selling. Expect to carry some inventory, no matter what the product is, but also understand that your choice of goods will have some effect on how much you'll need to shell out upfront. Schwartz was buying surplus apparel, so $700 gave him plenty to work with for the first few months. When a Florida-based husband-wife team founded their telecommunications firm, on the other hand, they invested about $2,400 to

> ## Smart Tip
> **Tip...**
>
> The early stages of business can be grueling, so be sure to keep enough personal money in reserve for yourself and your family to live on for six months. Keep this money separate from your business finances, and use it sparingly while your business is in the start-up phase.

The Distributor's Startup Shopping List

Everyone loves shopping lists, so here's one that you can use as a guideline for getting your distributorship up and running. You'll need:

In the office

- ❑ computer and printer
- ❑ fax machine (or a multifunction machine that serves as printer/fax/copier and more)
- ❑ telephone(s) with multiple phone lines and cell phone
- ❑ voice mail system
- ❑ online access via high-speed cable line
- ❑ office supplies (paper, pens, pencils, clipboards, etc.)

In the warehouse

- ❑ pallet or racking systems to hold the product
- ❑ forklift for moving goods
- ❑ a dock that delivery vehicles can back up to for loading and unloading goods
- ❑ your startup inventory (Read more about stocking up in Chapter 8 of this book.)

On the road

- ❑ truck, van, or other method of delivery (for distributors shipping out of their delivery area, this means setting up an account with a nationwide delivery firm such as UPS or Federal Express)
- ❑ lift-gate accessibility (even though you have a dock, your customers may not, so it's best to take your own lift-gate truck to their locations when making deliveries)

purchase a shipment of high-end telephones. And Benson—who sources one container-load of market baskets annually—invested a much more significant amount of money upfront (from her own pocket), but they didn't need any other inventory for the remainder of the year.

One of the best ways to determine affable inventory levels is by going back to some of the early market and customer research that you did before starting your business. That will show you what customers want and in what quantities. Then, as you grow your company, pay specific attention to the products, styles, and options that tend to "move faster" than other selections. If, for example, Benson knows that a turquoise market basket has been selling particularly well one year, she'll double up her order for the same item for her next container-load of goods.

Evan Money, president at wholesale extreme sports business Extreme Sports in Rancho Palos Verdes, California, takes a decidedly different approach to inventory and prefers to keep stock "as low as possible." In fact, he says shelling out a few extra dollars to drop-ship a rush, out-of-stock item to a customer next day is usually cheaper than carrying inventory that doesn't sell.

> ### Dollar Stretcher
>
> If you don't want to invest in large delivery trucks right out of the gate, try using delivery vans instead (such as the Honda Odyssey or the Chrysler Town and Country). They're roomy, less expensive, and much more economical than delivery trucks when it comes to fuel consumption.

"Margins in the wholesale distribution business are pretty low to begin with," says Money, "and I've become a big fan of having zero inventory. A lot of companies want to go big and stock up, but after years of working in the distribution field I can tell you that the ends just don't justify the means."

Getting Profitable

When it comes to securing financing, there's more to figuring out a number than just adding up the amount of equipment you'll need to get started. You'll also need to figure out how long it's going to take you to recoup the money you're investing or borrowing and how long it will be before you're in the black.

At Mikovch's wholesale wine distributorship, figuring out how much inventory he needed to meet his financial goals was easy. The entrepreneur used this simple formula:

Average wholesale price of a case of wine	$80
Hypothetical sales goal	$100,000
Inventory needed (divide the goal by the price of wine)	1,250 cases

The 1,250 figure dictates the amount of inventory that the distributor will have to sell to reach that sales goal. With Mikovch's gross profit margin (the amount of money left over after the product has been paid for) at 35 percent (at the high end for wholesale distribution), the formula reveals an average profit of $28 per case, or $35,000 annually, based on the example above.

Mikovch adds that wholesale distributors who are able to spend a lot of time on their businesses, rather than outsourcing tasks to other companies, can reach those profit margins without much effort. "We have no middleman between ourselves and the manufacturer, and no brokers—both of which can raise your wholesale prices from the manufacturers," he says.

Don't forget that wholesale distributors bring a lot more to the table than just facilitating the transfer of product from manufacturer to end user. For more information on value-added services in the distribution field, refer back to Chapter 2 of this book.

Looking for Financing

OK. You have rough estimates of how much money you need and how much you can make as a wholesale distributor. Now it's time to secure some financing.

For starters, you'll need to take a look at your own financial situation and determine how to tap into it without going broke in the process. It's a well-known fact that some entrepreneurs start their businesses on their personal credit cards (although we certainly don't advise this, it's worked for some) and with their savings.

If you're fortunate enough to have $50,000 or so to sink into your wholesale distribution business, then go for it. However, be sure that you consult with any other account holders or family members before doing so.

Schwartz is one distributor who enjoys outsourcing work to other companies instead of keeping it in-house. Unfortunately, the banks don't seem to share his enthusiasm. When making loans, he says, many financial institutions take into consideration assets (machinery, equipment, real estate, etc.) and liabilities like employees. For the entrepreneur working from the basement of his home and outsourcing functions like delivery, relabeling of products, and other duties, proving that you have assets is tough at best. Schwartz simply points the banks to his bottom line. He explains: "I tell them, look—do you care that I have a lot of machinery and equipment and that my profits are $50,000 a year, or would you prefer to see me outsourcing those functions and making $500,000 a year? I've found that from the bank's perspective, they actually are happier with the machinery."

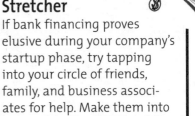

Dollar Stretcher

If bank financing proves elusive during your company's startup phase, try tapping into your circle of friends, family, and business associates for help. Make them into official investors in your firm, and you'll be on your way to success!

To solve the problem of raising money, many new wholesale distributors rely on self-financing during the startup phase. Those costs can range from just a few hundred dollars to hundreds of thousands of dollars, depending on the complexity of the business, how much overhead is needed at the outset, and the products themselves.

Regardless of whom you plan to approach for financing assistance—a bank, family member, or business associate—develop a business plan for your new company first. This plan, which includes a competitive analysis, information on market strategies, and financial facts, serves as the backbone for any new company seeking startup funds.

In the next chapter, we'll start hunting down a home for your new company. Whether you're going to start in your spare bedroom or in a 40,000-square-foot warehouse, you'll find out how to pick the right community, site, and facility for your new distribution firm.

Bright Idea

In search of bank financing? Check out your small community banks first. These financial institutions have been bragging about their ability to truly service the small-business customer, the one who is often overlooked by larger banks that are chasing big-dollar clients. (For the SBA's list of the 100 most active SBA 7(a) lenders, visit www.sba.gov/category/lender-navigation/lender-loan-data/100-most-active-sba-7a-lenders.)

Finding a Home for Your Company

When it comes to distribution, the old adage "location, location, location" holds true in some cases but certainly doesn't apply across the board. And while it is quite possible to start a small wholesale distribution business from just about anywhere, entrepreneurs who want to grow and prosper must at least be situated near transportation centers, especially if they plan to utilize shipping methods other than local delivery. Several other factors also come into play, so you'll want to read on to learn exactly what steps you'll need to take to secure the right location for your company.

Prime Locations for Wholesale Distributorships

Wholesale distributorships usually do not require high-traffic or high-visibility locations, but those that aren't homebased would be wise to find commercial space somewhere in the industrial section of town. Distributors should seek out areas that are rich in industry and close to transportation centers—especially if they are going to be shipping outside a 50-mile radius of their locations (this is the "normal" delivery area for most distributors, though the radius varies by company).

According to Pembroke Consulting's Adam Fein, desirable locations also vary by the type of product being distributed. "If you're an industrial distributor, for example, you'll want to be set up where the U.S. industrial base is, typically in the Midwestern states like Ohio, Michigan, Missouri, etc.," he advises. "Generally, however, wholesale distribution companies tend to locate where land is not too expensive and where they can buy or rent affordable warehouse space for the storage of inventory."

Fein adds that, for the most part, wholesale distributors are not located in downtown shopping areas. Instead, most are found "off the beaten path." If, for example, your company is a construction supply distributor that serves building or electrical contractors, your location will need to be accessible to those customers as they go about their daily routines.

The Right Site

Naturally, not every distributor needs a 40,000-square-foot warehouse situated in a major industrial park. In fact, location may not be a critical issue for the small wholesale distributorship where customers rarely visit. However, any distributor who plans to sell "over the counter" to customers—or have a walk-in showroom of some sort—would be wise to put some thought into his or her location.

Dollar Stretcher

If you can't afford warehouse space, try placing an ad in your local newspaper in search of "shared space." There are companies out there that aren't making full use of their warehouses, and some may be willing to lease you a portion of space where you can store your goods.

Let's Make a Deal

Because your building lease is the biggest long-term commitment you'll have to make when starting your business, Alexandria, Virginia, wine distributor Don Mikovch says to check out multiple sites and get prices on all of them. Then, pick the one you want and try to leverage your offers against one another. For example: If building A is the best candidate but more expensive than building B by $1 per square foot, try offering building A's owner 50 cents less per square foot and justify it by telling him of your interest in building B and its lower price. Of course, this negotiating tactic isn't win-win for the landlord, so its success will depend heavily on the demand for commercial warehouse space in your area.

Another consideration when looking at prospective locations is leasehold improvements. In other words, anyone who wants to lease a building and then build it out to meet their requirements (e.g., add pallet racking, additional docking bays, etc.) should lease for a minimum of five years to really make use of those improvements.

Finally, a good strategy for distributors is retain the right to sublease the building in case his or her company grows out of the building during the lease term. That way, the distributorship won't lose money if it moves out early.

It's important to note that the location of your business should be decided based on accessibility and visibility (for the customer) and affordability (for the company itself). Be sure to check out your county or city zoning laws before getting into a lease or purchasing a building—you don't want to find out too late that the location wasn't zoned for your type of business.

Study your target market, and make sure that your location of choice fully meets those clients' needs. For some companies, that means setting up shop in a high-foot-traffic area. For others, it means positioning their locations near public transportation. It can take time to find the perfect location for your business, so get an early start and don't give up.

Mike Smeaton of the Safety Market Group, a buying group of 50 independent safety equipment distributors in Brooksville, Florida, says a new distributor's location is best determined by available, affordable warehouse space that has adequate logistic support (such as UPS and FedEx) and available skilled employees. "Most wholesale distributors are not retail-oriented, so foot traffic is not as important as square footage cost," says Smeaton.

▲

Home Court Advantage

Wholesale distribution is a versatile business. Because most of the time you'll be delivering products to your customers as opposed to having them come to you (though some distributors do have walk-up counters and storefronts), the average customer won't really know or care about where that product is stored. For this reason, using your basement, garage, or spare bedroom as a starting point in business can make perfect sense, as long as it's situated near transportation hubs where products can be shipped and received on a daily (or more frequent) basis

A new wholesale distributor can certainly start from home, but whether he or she succeeds there ultimately depends on the product. So where a garage could certainly warehouse a jewelry or gift business, for example, if you're selling heavy equipment you'll probably need more "official" space for your operations. Oftentimes, a distributor may start from home and then move into a separate location when the firm outgrows the homebased setup.

> ## Bright Idea
> As you search for your company's starter home, don't overlook your garage. Many wholesale distributors have moved their cars out into the driveway and made ample room for their new company right in their garages. Set up a desk and computer in the corner and you have the perfect makeshift warehouse—all with a super-low overhead cost.

> ## Smart Tip
> *Tip...*
> Homebased entrepreneurs in search of a location where they can negotiate with customers in person would be wise to check out the various office suites and meeting rooms in their areas. There, you can plop down a fee and meet with customers in a professional setting, away from your home office or warehouse.

Lease, Rent, or Buy?

If you decide to set up your company in a commercial location, you'll have three choices: lease space, rent space, or buy the building. For the most part, your decision will be between leasing and buying because, quite frankly, the owners will want you to occupy the space for at least a few years (renting is more of a short-term option). This can pose a problem for you in the very early stages, namely because you are never quite sure how quickly your business will—or, in some cases, will not—grow. While purchase prices for commercial locations vary greatly, lease rates for warehouses (which also vary by geographical location) range from $6 to $15 and up per square foot.

Don Mikovch, president of Alexandria, Virginia-based Borvin Beverage, recommends that all new wholesale distributors lease space whenever possible. He explains why. "One of the wonderful things about wholesaling, versus other manufacturing and retailing businesses, is that wholesaling locations are much less expensive. After all, you just need a flat-floor warehouse. It's not like a meat-processing plant, for example, where they have to have equipment like pulleys installed in the ceiling in order to operate properly."

Other distributors may feel differently. If the capital is available, for example, it may be smarter to go ahead and purchase the facilities. Don't forget to factor future value into your decision. For instance, if you want to be near a planned shopping center or close to a place where two highways meet, you may realize that those areas can become much more valuable and that the rents might eventually go up. However, if you own the building from the outset, then you don't have to worry about it, and it becomes an asset for your business.

These days, location is becoming less and less of an issue for the entrepreneur looking to start a business. As the internet has broken down barriers between large and small companies, and as professional voice mail services, marketing materials, and other tools formerly for highly capitalized firms become easy to acquire on a small budget, it's now easier than ever to start a business from a spare bedroom. The average wholesale distribution firm can be started up anywhere, as long as there are manufacturers to buy from and customers to sell to.

In the next chapter, we'll give you the lowdown on exactly what you're going to need for your company's new home, including office equipment, distribution-related equipment, and a method of delivery for your products.

Setting Up
Shop

Once you've found a home for your new company, it's time to start thinking about how you're going to build it out to meet your needs. Building out includes the addition of equipment and other necessities to your warehouse, home, or other location to facilitate the shipping, receiving, and storage of goods.

The Bare Necessities

How you set up your wholesale distribution business's interior is highly dependent on what type of product you're selling, the kind of facility it's housed in, and the methods of shipping and receiving you're utilizing. For example, the homebased entrepreneur selling small hand tools from his garage would probably need the following:

- Shelving units or some other storage and organizational implements
- Room for office space (details on setting up your office will follow later in this chapter)
- A method of getting the goods in and out of the garage (a sturdy, wheeled hand truck will do the trick for small boxed items)

On the other hand, the entrepreneur who leases warehouse space for the wholesale distribution of, say, automobile tires would need:

- Pallet racking and an appropriate number of pallets on which to store the tires
- A forklift for moving the tires into their respective positions, then removing them when the time comes to ship them to customers

It Adds Up

Here are some approximate price ranges to help you figure out how much money you'll need to get your company up and running. We've based the prices on the needs of a hypothetical 5,000-square-foot warehouse.

	Low End	High End
Pallet racking (10 rows or sections)	$4,000	$25,000
Pallets	$55 each	N/A
Forklift (new)	$50,000	$75,000
Forklift (used)	$5,000	$15,000
Pallet truck (a piece of equipment used instead of a forklift to move pallets)	$500	$1,500
Shelving (10 rows or sections)	$1,000	$10,000
Hand truck	$75	$150
Office equipment (including basic PC, fax machine, telephone, etc.)	$1,000	$5,000
Office furniture (desk, chair, filing cabinets)	$500	$1,500

- Room for office space
- A loading dock to facilitate shipping and receiving

While it may appear that the business of tires is more capital-intensive than that of small hand tools, a supervisor in a Florida-based wholesale tire distribution center assures us that it's not. He explains, "We know of a few local distribution centers that have the tires literally stacked on the floor. However, they do a lot less volume than we do, so it's a system that works well for them." (For more information on what it will take to get your wholesale distribution business up and running, refer back to "The Distributor's Startup Shopping List" on page 37.)

Standard Office Equipment

In addition to the necessary specialized equipment, your company is also going to need some basic office equipment and a safe place to house it. This space needs to be out of the way of forklifts, roaming eyeballs, and other hazards. At home, this probably won't be much of an issue because you can keep your office in the house and your products in either the garage or the basement. However, if the warehouse you're leasing doesn't have a separate office in it, you'll probably want to build one for yourself. This will take up 60 to 80 square feet, partitioned off by four walls, in the corner of the warehouse and near electrical outlets and phone jacks.

In your office, you'll need a sturdy desk, ergonomically correct office chair, telephone, fax capabilities (either a traditional machine or an online service like eFax), and filing cabinets to store any paper-based orders, check stubs, and other necessary pieces of information. To increase your mobility, invest in a tablet computer like an iPad or Android and sign up for the many different free business and productivity apps that these tools have to offer.

If you're serving a customer base that's located outside your local calling area, you may also want to sign up for a toll-free number. Don't forget a good customer relationship management software (CRM) program, a cloud-based storage system like Dropbox (for transferring large files and photos to and from customers and business partners), and a good calendar system (like Google Calendar) for keeping track of your appointments and deadlines.

Smart Tip

Tip...

Don't forget to hook up an additional phone line for your new business, even if you run it out of your garage. It makes good sense taxwise because you can then write off all expenses for that new line. And don't forget to invest in a good-quality voice mail system that can handle your after-hours calls.

When Keith Schwartz, president of wholesale tie and belt distributor On Target Promotions in Warrensville Heights, Ohio, started his business, he was lucky enough to already own a phone, computer, and fax machine. He created what he refers to as "fancy letterhead" by having an artist draw the company's name for him and then copying it onto blank paper. He was in business soon after that.

"That was it," Schwartz says. "I had saved one year's worth of income, and that was the amount of startup cash that I had to work with." Depending on how many resources you have, you may be able to find used office furniture rather than buy everything new.

In terms of computing power, at minimum, you'll need a PC with an operating system (most businesses use a Windows-based system although Macs are growing in popularity in the business world), traditional or cloud-based office software (spreadsheets, word processor, etc.), specialized software (if desired), and the necessary peripherals: a modem, printer, and scanner. There are myriad options when it comes to distribution software. (See the Appendix of this book for the names and contact information of software providers for the distribution industry.) Prices vary widely, but the basic functions that a distributor needs are accounting (including receivables, payables, and expense tracking) and inventory control.

> ## Bright Idea
>
> As a wholesale distributor, you'll probably be dealing with multiple vendors, all of whom will want to send you their literature and catalogs. To keep things organized, dedicate one filing cabinet to such materials and use alphabetized hanging folders, organized by product name, for easy accessibility when a customer calls and asks if you carry a particular product. With so many companies looking to streamline their operations via a paperless approach, you'll also want to be able to maintain all of your digital files in an accessible system.

Today's distributors rely heavily on computer hardware and software to track inventory, manage financial processes, and handle communications. Two particularly popular pieces of software (either used in a traditional "installed" setup or via the cloud) are Warehouse Management Systems (WMS) and Transportation Management Systems (TMS). The former manages the activities of products and employees within the four walls of the warehouse, and the latter oversees movement of freight from the dock door and out to the customer's location.

Salespeople out in the field are more efficient when equipped with laptops and cell phones, for example, while accounting personnel are able to make quicker decisions—about new lines of customer credit, for example—when the information is at their fingertips. For this reason, all new distributors should invest in a system that can handle accounts receivable, accounts payable, and general ledger functions. A basic office system (such as Microsoft Office) is also necessary, as is a setup that can track and record inventory. Don't be afraid to invest in a few of those packages and be sure to check out the enterprise resource planning (ERP) options available for distributors. Once extremely expensive and cumbersome, many of these systems are now cloud-based and can handle just about any aspect of a distributor's operations.

Get those Wheels Rolling

In addition to your investments in a great location and the equipment necessary for getting it running smoothly, you'll also need to consider how necessary delivery vehicles will be. From there, whether you lease or buy your wheels is up to you. Generally, a leased vehicle requires less of a down payment. However, at the end of the lease, you turn in a vehicle that you've paid for and maintained for five or so years in exchange for . . . well, nothing. There are tax advantages to leasing vehicles, however, in that businesses can basically write off all expenses related to the truck, van, or car. It may be best to sit down with your accountant to figure out which method is best for you.

At Don Mikovch's Alexandria, Virginia-based wholesale wine distributorship, he says he finds it "easier to just buy" his company vehicles. His company started out small, however, and took a different route than most beverage distributors when it came to selecting a delivery vehicle: Rather than buy a large truck, he chose to buy a minivan. He explains: "One day I saw one of my competitors' trucks with the back door open. The truck contained about 60 cases of wine, but it was 90 percent empty." Today, Mikovch says he still uses the minivans for regional distribution—and his competitors have followed suit. "They're more maneuverable than trucks are, and most are more cost-effective in terms of fuel," he explains.

Beware!
Leasing a company vehicle for five years may mean investing more and getting less back, especially if you've signed a separate maintenance agreement that inevitably forces you to buy the newer model to avoid high maintenance costs. To avoid this problem, give your lease contract a thorough examination and voice any concerns with the manufacturer before signing.

Whether a new distributorship company leases or buys its vehicles is highly dependent on the amount of capital it has on hand. Unless you have deep pockets, you will probably end up leasing vehicles. In most cases, a startup firm should start out with one delivery vehicle, then add on as the business volume grows.

In the end, whether you lease or buy depends on your individual needs, what type of financing you have, and how long you plan to keep the vehicles or equipment in question. Be cautious when signing any long-term contracts, and realize that the equipment may become obsolete (especially computers, which are being upgraded at the speed of light) before the lease expires.

In the next chapter, we'll look at what type of inventory you'll need to get your business underway, where to find the merchandise to stock your shelves, and how to get it into your customers' hands.

Inventory
Matters

In today's competitive business arena, companies are on perpetual diets. Owners and managers strive to run the leanest possible companies with the fewest employees and least amount of inventory and liabilities. In the distribution sector, some companies are being run with very low inventories—thus reducing their major sale (nonequipment) investments.

▲

Others choose to stock up in order to have "just what the customer ordered" on hand when the need arises.

There are caveats to both strategies. For starters, when a company chooses not to stock up, it runs the risk of being out of an item when the customer comes calling. At the same time, the distributors who overstock can find themselves in a real pickle if they can't get rid of merchandise they thought they could unload easily.

Being a distributor is all about "turning" inventory (selling everything you have in stock and then replenishing it)—the more times you can turn your inventory in a year, the more money you will make. Get the most turns by avoiding stocking items that may end up sitting in your warehouse for more than 90 days.

Luckily, there is a happy medium. Read on to find out how to balance the scales just enough to keep your company profitable and your customers happy.

Stocking Up or Not?

How much inventory you buy at startup is going to depend heavily on exactly what you're selling, how far away your customers are located, and how demanding they are. For example, if you're supplying customers within a 20-mile radius of your warehouse with janitorial goods like paper towels, rubber gloves, and hand soap, then you can base your stocking quantities on the number of customers multiplied by an average usage by each. Their usage is most easily determined by asking them just how much they normally procure on a monthly basis.

On the other hand, if you are servicing a varied customer base located in different geographic areas, you may need to stock a little more than the entrepreneur in the previous example. Because you probably won't be visiting those customers at their locations, it may take a few months before you can determine just how much product they will be buying from you on a regular basis. Of course, you must also leave some breathing room for the "occasional" customer—the one who buys from you once a year and who will probably always catch you off guard. The good news is that having relationships with vendors can help fill those occasional needs quickly, even overnight or on the same day, if necessary.

In today's "lean" business world, one of the biggest mistakes a company can make is investing in more inventory that it really needs—or,

> **Smart Tip**
> Before investing in any inventory, do some thorough research on the marketplace. Instead of operating in a vacuum and assuming that you'll be able to unload whatever you can put your hands on, get some advice from manufacturers, customers, and even competitors in the industry. You may be surprised by what you find out!

that it can sell within a reasonable period of time. Inevitably, this costly inventory winds up gathering dust in a warehouse. In some cases, this occurs because the wholesale distributor didn't factor in its customers' wants and needs. Without these key metrics, companies wind up using a "seat of the pants" approach to inventory, hoping that their upfront investments pay off. A better bet is to keep your inventory approach as lean as possible without running out of stock, particularly on high-demand items. Achieving this balance may take a few tries, but within no time at all you'll be a pro at it if you put the time and energy into making it happen.

At Keith Schwartz's wholesale belt and tie distributorship in Warrensville Heights, Ohio, all it took was a $700 investment in closeout ties to get started. He resold them to a drugstore, pocketed the profits and reinvested the money in more inventory. It's a simple formula and one that works well for the small startup entrepreneur who is operating with low overhead.

Using Flash Inventory Reports

As an attorney who works often with startup wholesale distributors and who has also run his own hair accessories distributorship, Nat Wasserstein of Lindenwood Associates in Upper Nyack, New York, says flash reports are valuable tools that all distributors should have in their toolkits. "In my opinion, a company can be run using a single sheet of paper," says Wasserstein. By definition, he says a flash report is simply a snapshot of a company's current receivables, inventory levels, sales, and outstanding debt.

"Run this report every Monday and you'll not only know exactly where you stand, but you'll be able to adjust accordingly without having to wait until the end of the month or quarter to figure out something is wrong," says Wasserstein. This simple exercise can help distributors make financially savvy inventory and stocking decisions. Knowing that a large order of items reserved for a particular customer was recently cancelled and now available for sale, for example, means salespeople can get to work selling those items to other buyers (rather than letting them gather dust in the warehouse and "hoping beyond hope" that the original order comes back to life).

"Every Monday you should know what receivables are outstanding, who owes you what, which orders are open/closed, and how much money you have on hand," says Wasserstein. "On the inventory side, use your flash report to keep close tabs on what's in stock, what orders are outstanding, what's shipping this week, and so far. Then, use that matrix of data points to connect all of the dots within your business and to make the best possible decisions for the coming week."

The distributor who has already invested in a location, vehicles, and other necessities should also factor product life cycle into the inventory equation. Those with longer life cycles (hand tools, for example) are usually less risky to stock, while those with shorter life cycles (food, for example, usually has a short life cycle) can become a liability if there are too many of them on the shelf. The shorter the life cycle, the less product you'll want to have on hand. Ultimately, your goal will be to sell the product before having to pay for it. In other words, if you are buying computers, and if the manufacturer offers you 30-day payment terms, then you'll want to have less than 30 days' worth of inventory on the shelf. That way, you never end up "owning" the inventory and instead serve as a middleman between the company that's manufacturing and/or selling the product and the one that's buying it.

To sum up the tricks to stocking a wholesale distributorship:

- Don't overdo it when it comes to buying inventory.
- Try to grasp your customers' needs before you invest in inventory.
- If you can get away with doing it cheaply at first (especially those with low overhead), then go for it.
- Be wary of investing too much in short-lifecycle products, which you may get stuck with if they don't sell right away.
- Stock up to a level where you can sell the product before you have to pay for it.

Going Straight to the Source

No wholesale distributorship would be able to function without good sources of product, which are usually either manufacturers or other distributors. The number of vendors you deal with depends on how varied your own offerings are, how efficient (timely deliveries, good prices, nice to deal with, etc.) the individual vendors are, and how picky your customers are about brand (for example, you may need to deal with a specific manufacturer or distributor if you have a large-volume customer who will only buy a particular brand of hardhats for a construction site).

Keith Schwartz cautions new distributors against becoming too reliant on just a few suppliers and says that at the outset, his own firm became reliant on one supplier and one customer for 80 percent of its business. "Five months after I left my full-time job, the supplier stopped supplying me the products," he says. "I was dead in the water." To solve the problem, Schwartz changed the focus of his company from one that bought

Beware!
Before signing any exclusive partnering contracts with vendors or customers, consult with an attorney.

Howdy, Partner!

For years, companies have made decisions concerning where to buy parts, supplies, and services based solely on price. Times have changed. Today, these very companies are turning their attention to what consultants refer to as "relationship marketing" to meet the challenges of boosting profits, increasing market share, and enhancing competitive position in an increasingly global and cost-conscious marketplace.

The process, which calls for building long-term connections to suppliers and customers, is making companies rethink their whole approach to purchasing and selling. Effective partnering is accomplished through well-established, long-term relationships; a concentration on win-win relationships that benefit both parties; and by working together as true business partners, instead of simply acting like vendors and customers.

Here's the trick for wholesale distributors: Rather than focusing on price alone, scrutinize more closely from whom you're buying, what you're buying, how you buy and what you're paying. By partnering with key vendors to reduce costs, wholesale distributors have managed to save money on their bills for purchased goods. In addition, many distributors, who are essentially acting as suppliers to their own customers, are using the same tactics and forming similar relationships with their valued customer base.

salesmen's samples to one that bought product directly from manufacturers. "I relied on my ability to sell consumer products and started to sell for small manufacturers that needed help in my geographic territory," he says. "Eventually, I increased my cash flow and got back on my feet." Most wholesale distributors spend their time trying to perfect the balance between vendor and customer. To find good vendors, distributors should visit industry trade shows, read trade magazines (both articles and advertisements), and approach manufacturers directly. Often, the best chance to represent a product line will come if your distributorship is in a region where a manufacturer has poor or no representation. Check each manufacturer out carefully before taking on its lines, and remember that your own reputation will be affected by

Bright Idea

Trade shows are a great place to meet up with manufacturers and other suppliers in a setting where you can view their products and catalogs and talk to their sales reps. Flip through your industry's trade magazine, or contact an industry trade group for information on upcoming shows.

Bright Idea

When deciding on shipping methods, don't overlook the fact that many manufacturers will "drop ship" (ship directly to customers on your behalf) product for you, especially for rush shipments.

the product quality and the service provided by the supply sources you select.

Once you've found a few good sources of product, the next step will be to establish a working relationship with them. Translation: You need to establish credit with your sources. Because distributors usually have to wait 10 to 30 days to be paid by their own customers (typical invoice terms are net 30 days), they must negotiate similar or better terms with their suppliers to avoid paying out money they don't have. The solution is to establish credit with your suppliers.

That's exactly what Beth Shaw did when opening YogaFit Inc. in Los Angeles, California, in 1994. Knowing that her customers were in need of quality-made, innovative yoga mats, apparel, and exercise equipment, she sought out suppliers who made such items at reasonable prices. She searched both domestically and overseas for the goods and today includes a mix of both in her product lineup. "Sourcing great product is something we do on an ongoing basis," says Shaw, who is also always on the lookout for other companies to partner with and do business with. When publisher Random House began expanding into lifestyle, diet, and nutrition topics for the books, for example, Shaw stepped up to the plate to write her own tome on the yoga lifestyle. She also recently signed a deal with Snap Fitness to license the YogaFit name for fitness franchise studios nationally. "I continue to partner with people in ancillary industries for growth opportunities and just be much more mindful of new opportunities," says Shaw, "while at the same time looking to source less expensive products that enable a higher markup. At this point, we're really cautious about not buying products where we don't have a decent markup."

To avoid potential conflict, thoroughly research your market prior to making any decisions about what products you're going to sell. (Read more about market research in Chapter 3.)

From Supplier to Customer

The next critical step in setting up your business is to establish a few relationships with

Smart Tip

Tip...

Remember that you'll have to extend credit to your customers. Doing so puts you even more in the role of the "middleman" who could wind up in a situation where customers are paying late and vendors are expecting to be paid for orders on time. Be sure to factor this into your cash flow strategy as a distributor.

freight carriers and shipping companies. Even if you're only delivering to your local area, you should always be prepared to handle things like incoming shipments that aren't handled properly by the manufacturer, local customers who may want a big shipment sent 1,000 miles away, and other situations that can crop up.

For Shaw, who ships product worldwide, freight costs vary by location and timeliness of delivery. The majority of the products are shipped via UPS or FedEx, which offer discounted rates to bulk shippers.

To set up relationships with carriers (including overnight companies like FedEx, ground shipping companies like UPS, and over-the-road trailers like SAIA), it's simply a matter of calling their local office and setting up a business account. After a credit and reference check, the company will set up a merchant account for you and will either stop at a regular time each day or when you call them, depending on the frequency of shipments. Be sure to investigate liability coverage, in case a package gets lost. You may need additional insurance.

Another major trend that has taken hold in the distribution industry over the last ten years is drop shipping—or, the delivery of goods directly to a customer either from a manufacturer or from a third-party logistics (3PL) provider. Benson, for example, contracts with a local warehouse that not only stores her company's market baskets, but that also picks and packs the items and sends them directly to the customers who ordered them. "I basically don't even have to touch the products," says Benson, whose sole employee provides support when it's time to staff up a farmer's market or trade show booth. "Other than that, I pretty much just outsource everything and then handle the rest of the operations myself."

Benson isn't alone. According to Brandon Delgrosso, president and CEO, at Doba, a Utah-based firm that specializes in drop-shipping for wholesale distributors, the number of distributors using drop shipping has increased from 24 percent to 41 percent between 2013 and 2014. "That's a major jump in the number of companies that are finally realizing that they want to tap into this opportunity," says Delgrosso, who sees increased pressure from retailers and online selling platforms like Overstock as one of the driving factors. "Overstock is just one firm that wants 90 percent of its orders drop shipped in its efforts to cut back on warehousing its own products."

Now that we've covered many of the operational, equipment, and inventory issues involved in starting up a wholesale distribution firm, we'll move into new territory: human capital. In the next chapter, we'll give you details on how to attract and retain the right employees to help you run your new company.

Finding the Rest
of Your Team

f it were humanly possible, most entrepreneurs would stick to running one-person operations. Unfortunately, this would severely inhibit company growth and at the same time completely burn out the average business owner. For these reasons, it's wise to consider hiring employees as your company grows.

If your wholesale distribution firm started out as a one-person operation, then your first new hire will probably be a jack-of-all-trades type of assistant who can mimic many of your own moves. As your firm grows, you can add more specialized positions like warehouse manager, sales representatives, and office staff.

Staffing the Right Way

Once your wholesale distribution company gets up and running, you will want to hire employees as it becomes necessary. How will you know when it's necessary? Well, when your employees start wearing more than five hats, or when you realize that working 24 hours a day wouldn't even help you get caught up, you know it's time to hire help.

For starters, you'll want someone who can manage customer relations. This person will handle inbound and outbound telephone calls to customers, as well as emails, texts, social media messages, and letters to and from customers regarding issues, concerns, and questions. Good candidates include recent college graduates and individuals who already have some sales experience. Seek out aggressive workers who can not only help boost company sales but also be sensitive to customer needs.

Next up on the hiring list will be someone who can run your company's finance department. Their duties will include verifying customer credit, working with third-party organizations (leasing companies, for example) and handling other finance-related issues for the company. This person should have a financial background or credit management experience.

As you begin to delegate more responsibilities to your employees, you'll also need to determine who is going to handle the purchasing function. When the time comes to hire someone specifically for purchasing, that person will find himself or herself working directly with your vendors to negotiate prices and delivery time frames. He or she will also manage the inventory in your warehouse or distribution center. Another consideration, which may or may not be necessary, depending on where you're located and how much of your business is done by referral, will be a marketing professional. This person

> ## Smart Tip
> **Tip...**
>
> Giving up control isn't easy, but your business can't grow if you don't hire employees. Take it slow, and handpick your new workers carefully. In the long run, you'll be glad you relinquished certain duties to others so you can concentrate on the tasks you enjoy!

should be experienced in the field and will be responsible for presenting your company to your customer base, vendors, media, trade groups, and other entities in a positive fashion.

Once your front office is staffed, you'll need to hire a few warehouse associates who will physically take inventory off of the shelf, pack it in boxes, and receive incoming inventory. They will also operate the forklifts in the warehouse and handle other tasks as needed. Depending on how your company is set up, you'll probably need a warehouse manager as well. This person should have some warehouse experience and will spend most of his or her time worrying about control and efficiency and making sure workers are filling orders correctly. At Borvin Beverage, Don Mikovch's wholesale wine distributorship

Beware!

Don't neglect to check the references on your prospective employee's resume before making a decision to hire him or her. It's easy to make a fancy-looking resume these days. Dig down past the fluff and make sure the job experience is as solid as it looks on paper.

in Alexandria, Virginia, for example, his warehouse manager ensures that the right wine is put into the right cases for the customer, that the trucks are loaded, and that the delivery people are on time in delivering it.

How Much You'll Have to Pay

Pay rates for employees in the distribution field vary greatly by geographic area. As with any other type of business, for example, a warehouse in midtown Chicago will probably pay more for workers than would a warehouse located in a rural Iowa town.

On average, an office manager or assistant will demand $15 to $30 per hour, depending on experience. Professional positions (purchasing or marketing associates, for example) will command a starting yearly salary in the $30,000 to $40,000 range. The exact salary level varies by geography, with most entry-level associates commanding a salary somewhere in the $30,000 range, with a slightly more experienced associate commanding more.

Salaries paid to warehouse workers are also dictated by geographic location and what other businesses are nearby. According to Keith Schwartz, salaries for workers "vary greatly based on whether you're in an urban or metropolitan market." He pays workers the going hourly rate for their positions and lets them choose their own hours. "We attract great, loyal workers because larger companies with bigger warehouses may pay more per hour for them, but we are extremely flexible," Schwartz says. "This was great while we were a small company, but today we're much less flexible and require full-time and overtime workers. We also pay more."

On average, warehouse workers command anywhere from minimum wage to $10 per hour to start. Pay rates for office personnel range from $10 to $17 per hour, depending on experience, and warehouse managers generally earn $30,000 per year and up, depending on their experience in the field.

Alternatives to Traditional Employees

If the numbers listed above sound like a lot to shell out during the startup phase, there are alternatives. These days, nontraditional work styles are common and tend to be flexible. For example, you can outsource your credit department to a firm that specializes in such functions. There are even "virtual assistants" that you can hire on a per-project basis via the internet, and you don't even need to provide desk space for them!

You can find virtual assistants by searching on a site like oDesk (www.odesk.com), Virtual Staff Finder (www.virtualstafffinder.com), or Evirtualservices (www.evirtualservices.com). You can also do a general search online for "virtual assistant" + your specific line of work or industry, if you need specialized help.

This Is How We Do It

One might assume that a wholesale wine distributorship would want to hire salespeople who know something about wine. Not a wine expert, of course, but at least someone who knows the difference between their zinfandels and their chardonnays.

Not at Borvin Beverage, Don Mikovch's Alexandria, Virginia-based wholesale wine distributorship. In fact, he says he won't even interview a prospective salesperson who presents himself or herself as a "connoisseur of wine."

"We want salespeople who say 'Yeah, this is wine, but it might as well be ice cubes,'" says Mikovch. "They need to be completely unattached from the product." In addition to the detachment, he also looks for drive in his salespeople and sales experience in a variety of industries.

When it comes to hiring for other positions, Mikovch says he looks for different traits. In administrative workers, for example, he's seeking "KSA," or knowledge, skill, and attitude. "They're the type of employee you want to stay in the office and worry about the numbers, the follow-up letters, and the taxes," he says. "My job as an executive is to hire one type of person for sales and a completely different person to be, say, an office manager."

Mikovch concurs: "The warehouse is one area where we've found contract associates to be very effective. As our business goes through cycles, we're able to fill in with temporary workers. We use them in positions that don't require a long learning curve—where we can quickly train them and get them up to speed."

Schwartz also relies heavily on outsourcing rather than full-time employees. "Until a company is making $2 to $3 million in annual sales—and able to afford an executive and administrative staff—I truly believe that everything should be outsourced," he says. "Today we are above that mark and we do in fact have a complete staff."

Tips for Finding Employees

It's a problem companies of all sizes and across all industries experience at one time or another: You just can't keep good employees. In distribution, it's no different.

For the small entrepreneur to put months into training an employee only to have him or her leave for other jobs, can be truly devastating. To prevent this from happening too often (OK, even we know you can't keep it from happening sometimes!), try following these tips for recruiting and retaining employees:

- *Offer them enough money.* If a truck driver comes to you for a job and if he was already making $25 per hour, then you know that offering him $18 per hour won't work. Even if he does take the pay cut, he'll only leave when something better comes along. The solution? Stick to hiring employees who have been making the same or less than what you're willing to offer.

- *Explore their potential.* If you're looking for an administrative assistant who will remain your administrative assistant, then look for the appropriate credentials to fill that need. However, if you want an assistant who can be groomed into a salesperson and essentially "grow up" through your company, then look for the credentials that will meet the position's needs.

- *Search outside your area.* Try placing employment ads in newspapers outside your local area—preferably in an area with a higher unemployment rate, such as a city where a large plant may have recently shut down.
- *Cultivate, cultivate, cultivate.* Everyone wants to feel wanted, and that includes your employees. When you find a great warehouse worker or purchasing agent, be sure to foster their professional and personal growth by allowing them to share ideas and truly be a part of your growing organization.

As a wholesale distributor, the primary obstacle to finding and keeping good employees in a warehouse atmosphere is that you'll be competing with many other companies for the same skill sets. In other words, a warehouse worker would also make a good assembly line worker or auto detailer. The key is to choose carefully and to make your employees feel like they're part of a team and not just another laborer. The same goes for your sales staff and administrative personnel. Such jobs are adaptable across a variety of industries, so be sure to treat employees well, make them feel they're contributing to the overall success of the company, and listen to their needs.

Keeping Them Happy

It used to be that small startup firms could get away with not offering their employees health insurance. No longer. No longer. Today, everyone from the two-person operation to the 2,000-employee conglomerate offers some type of health insurance. Thanks to the Affordable Care Act, companies with 50 or more employees are now required to cover their employees. Businesses with 50 or fewer employees may get employee health coverage in the SHOP Marketplace. Employers of this size aren't required to offer health coverage, but they can use the Small Business Health Options Program (SHOP) to offer coverage to their employees. (For an FAQ on the SHOP Marketplace see: www.healthcare.gov/what-is-the-shop-marketplace/.)

The bottom line is this: once you start hiring employees, you'll need to offer some sort of health insurance. But it doesn't have to kill your budget. There are various trade organizations (see the Appendix of this book) you can join to get group rates, and you can also negotiate with

> **Bright Idea**
> If you're lucky enough to have a large, hard-working family (or extended family), then now is the time to tap into their strengths and put them to work for your new company.

What Employees Want

You may start out as a lone eagle, but to grow your firm, you're going to have to enlist the help of others to whom you can delegate tasks. At that point, your role will likely be transformed from "solo entrepreneur" to "manager" or "leader." According to SCORE's small-business consultants, here's what those employees will want from you as their leader:

○ *Employees want to trust you and for you to trust them.* Begin by being trustworthy and extending trust.

○ *Employees want good two-way communication.* Begin by being a good listener.

○ *Employees want to be challenged.* Set forth your vision and goals clearly and then let your workers exercise their creativity and authority in meeting your goals.

○ *Employees want accountability.* Not only should you hold them accountable for their own performance, but you should also measure your own performance.

○ *Employees want recognition.* Offer praise and express appreciation at every opportunity.

your employees on the percentage that each of you will pay. Most employees understand that a startup probably won't foot the entire bill, but dividing the costs 50/50 or even 75/25 can make it more fair. Down the road—as your business becomes profitable—you can review the agreement and renegotiate if necessary. (You might want to put a time frame on that promise if the employee is reluctant to pay their portion. Tell them you will renegotiate it in one year, for example.)

In the next chapter, we'll show you how to get word of your new company out to the rest of the world. We'll also give you an inside look at how wholesale distributors are using high-tech tools like the internet and ecommerce to expand their businesses and how they keep their customers coming back for more.

Getting the
Word Out

ow that you have the scoop on how to

staff your company and keep your employees happy and

healthy, it's time to get those customers beating down your

door. The majority of wholesale distribution firms work both in

a direct-selling fashion (calling, faxing, or emailing customers

to sell their wares) and by word of mouth (the referral system).

However, you can get a jump on your competitors by testing out some of the more advanced strategies we'll discuss in this chapter.

The Advertising Hook

When was the last time you saw an ad for a wholesale distribution company in your local newspaper? Probably never, and for good reason. Running a newspaper ad would mean shelling out too much money to reach too broad of an audience. Instead, you'll have to get more creative and ferret out the magazines and trade journals your potential customers are reading. For example, if you're distributing women's fashion accessories, then you'll want to advertise in places like More or Glamour, both of which cater to your audience. Distributors selling specialty gifts might try Smart Retailer, which targets small retailers of home décor and specialty items.

One of the most effective ways for distributors to advertise is through highly targeted ads directed at specific consumer demographics. For example, a distributor of technology components whose customer base includes computer resellers would advertise in publications that are specifically targeted at that customer base. And by utilizing action-based ads (those that include a strong call to action—call by a certain date and

---

Face Facts

It's a commonly known fact that most wholesale distributors choose not to advertise. In fact, the majority would rather do their business by word-of-mouth referrals, direct contact with customers, and cold-calling new prospects.

However, some wholesalers would like to advertise but simply can't. And it's not because of budgetary reasons—it's the law. Just ask Don Mikovch of Borvin Beverage, a wholesale wine distributorship in Alexandria, Virginia. In his state, advertising the sale of alcoholic beverages is illegal, so he relies solely on his outside sales team to get out and meet the customers in person.

While one would think that this barrier would hurt the wine wholesaler, Mikovch says quite the opposite is true. He explains, "It's actually kind of nice because we are a very small wholesale distributor, but we can be on par with our 100-year-old competitors who are making $40 to $50 million in sales annually. Nobody can advertise, so the playing field is completely leveled in that regard."

save 10 percent on your first order, for example), distributors can get the phone ringing by creating a sense of urgency.

While there is no "typical" advertising budget for wholesalers, namely because some firms just don't advertise, most firms set their advertising budgets based on a percentage of forecasted annual sales. The amount varies widely depending on the industry the distributor is in.

Keith Schwartz, who has started and run several wholesale distributorships over the year, says his firm uses a combination of the web, face-to-face selling and trade shows to get his customers interested in his products. Benson uses a combination of the web and a physical presence at farmer's markets to find and retain customers. Others still use door knocking, direct mail, and other more traditional means of garnering new customers. And while no "one size fits all" approach works for everyone, new distributors should try to think out of the box when it comes to advertising. Don't limit yourself to just trade magazines and radio ads, for example, but think of advertising as encompassing all activities that bring customers to your front door, telephone, website, or social networking platforms. Allocating 5 to 10 percent of your annual budget to efforts like custom signage, bulk mailers, and a localized advertising program (via an online venue like Google Places, for example) is a good starting point.

And remember that advertising could be sending a person out on the street to sell your products and get your message out. Whether it's putting feet on the street, sending out brochures, or putting an ad in the newspaper, on TV, or on the radio, at some level you are going to have to spend money on marketing and advertising in order to get customers to your online home or brick-and-mortar presence.

The PR and Promotions Game

It's a bit more time-consuming, but it's definitely less expensive than placing ads in magazines: It's called PR, or public relations, and it works. This strategy involves preparing press releases—announcing your new company, business milestones, or other newsy events—and sending them to your local radio, TV, and newspaper outlets, along with your industry's trade magazines. It's a strategy that requires much follow-up with editors, journalists, and publishers. However, just one media placement—at no charge—can pay for the efforts in one fell swoop.

Among the wholesale distributors we interviewed for this book, however, PR wasn't nearly as popular as promotions were. Most prefer to host special events and open houses to create goodwill, attract new customers, and make their existing customers feel special.

For example, Don Mikovch of Borvin Beverage says his company started the wine-tasting trend in his home state of Virginia back in 1987. As a small wholesale wine distributor of primarily specialty, high-end wines, he says he realized early on that his company would have to do something special to stand out from the crowd of heavily advertised Gallo and Inglenook wines crowding the grocery shelves. "We offered the wine tasting to our retailers during the high-traffic times—Friday evenings and Saturdays," he explains. "It really caught on, and now our big competitors are [doing] the same thing."

And it's not just Mikovch's competitors who took notice of the events' effectiveness. When a new supermarket in Virginia contacted him about doing wine tastings in a new store with a wine section on the second floor, accessible by elevator, he jumped on the opportunity. Says Mikovch, "This gave us the inroads to get our product lines on the shelves more easily than our competitors did because this store is not interested in the big-volume wines."

Hanging Out Your Shingle

Beware!
Don't throw your money away for an advertisement in a magazine that might not reach your targeted audience. Investigate by asking for a media kit from the magazine. This will give you the CPM (cost per thousand, or how much it costs you to reach 1,000 readers) of your advertisement, detailed information on the publication's readership, and other valuable information.

Because many startup wholesale distribution companies work from warehouses in industrial parks, small, out-of-the-way locations and even from home, signage is not usually an issue. For larger companies that have walk-up counters and storefronts, however, it's a different story. Such companies should have both a roadside sign (located at the front of the industrial park's entrance road, for instance) and a sizable sign on the building.

According to Merrifield, a good-sized sign with a company logo, placed on top of the warehouse or building, is very necessary for wholesale distributors. "It helps create branding and recognition," he says. Each of his company's locations includes a "will call" area that looks like a showroom. It includes samples of his firm's products, signage from various manufacturers, special offers, and promotional fliers. "It basically looks and feels like a store with merchandise," Merrifield adds. "In these 'will call' areas, customers can come in and make purchases in person."

Getting Social with Customers Online

Bright Idea

Here's an inexpensive way to promote your company: Compile a list of potential customers by using your local online advertising platforms, trade directories, social media sites, and other resources. Then create mailers or postcards (available at your local office supply store) announcing your new company and its offerings.

Social networking sites like Facebook, LinkedIn, Twitter, Instagram, and Pinterest make it easy (and free—other than the time spent) to connect with customers online without any cold calling or direct selling. Posting news about new styles on Facebook, re-tweeting useful and informational links on Twitter, and uploading new product photos to Pinterest can all go a long way in helping to spread the word about your company and its activities.

Another good way to leverage social networking platforms is by blogging – a fairly simple process of "posting" information online without having to spend hours a week on the task. Did you read an article in *The Wall Street Journal* that speaks directly to your audience? Pull the headline and the first paragraph or two from it, add a short explanation in your own words, link your post to the original site and voila! You have a blog post. Next, post information about your blog across all of your social networking platforms (a paid service like Hootsuite is viable way to tie them all together without having to post on every platform individually) as a way to engage your audience in your post. Invite readers to post comments about your post and respond accordingly (particularly if someone complains or rants). Over time, you'll amass a library of content (Google loves libraries of useful and relevant content!) that past, present, and future customers will visit and revisit regularly.

Keeping It Fresh

As you explore your options in the social networking realm, and as you add new platforms to your strategy, remember that it pays to update regularly and keep the content fresh. In other words, simply posting a few useful items and then waiting weeks to add more is a "set it and forget it" approach that doesn't work. Your customers are hungry

Smart Tip

Tip...

Don't forget that as a wholesale distributor, you'll be relying on both vendors and customers for your livelihood: One will be supplying product, and the other will be buying it. Technically, both are your "business partners," so be sure to treat them as such!

for information and if you don't provide a steady stream of it, they will look elsewhere for it.

A better approach is to assign at least one internal employee to be responsible for your social networking platforms. If this isn't feasible, consider outsourcing the task to a third party. Google the term "social media management" and you'll see that there are professionals out there who specialize in helping companies set up and maintain their Facebook, LinkedIn, Twitter, and other accounts. If third-party assistance isn't in your budget right now, check out a service like Hootsuite (www.hootsuite.com). This social media management dashboard allows you to develop content and then post it across all of your social media platforms at once.

It All Comes Down to Customer Service

We've given you the information you need to advertise and promote your new wholesale distribution business, but now we're going to share with you the real secret to winning customers. It can be summed up in three simple words: superior customer service. Without it, your business will not prosper. With it, your company will stand head and shoulders above the rest.

Because distribution customers rarely purchase from one distributor, finding and retaining customers is a daily task. Focus on developing strong relationships with customers, understanding their needs, and making sure they choose you for more than price and availability—both of which are of utmost importance to your customers. Distributors have broken down those barriers slightly over the past few years by offering more value-added services (such as plant assessments and light assembly work) to their customers. They've also beefed up customer service operations and focused on hiring employees who truly understand the value of building customer relationships.

While customer service certainly plays a major role in the success of any distributorship, the way the company presents itself to the rest of the

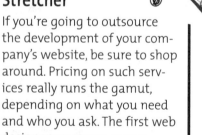

Dollar Stretcher

If you're going to outsource the development of your company's website, be sure to shop around. Pricing on such services really runs the gamut, depending on what you need and who you ask. The first web designer you come across might do great work, but the next might do acceptable work for a much lower price.

region, state, nation, or world is really what gets those customers in the door in the first place.

Whether you choose to advertise your business or simply rely on word-of-mouth referrals to bring in that business depends on your situation. Whatever your decision, you now have the marketing tools that will help your company get noticed. In the next chapter, we'll show you how to manage your finances, including handling sales taxes and other pertinent issues that go along with owning a wholesale distribution business.

Tip...

Smart Tip

If you are running your wholesale distribution business from a warehouse, be sure to mark the entrance to the office area clearly (above the door is fine) so that visitors who wander in can easily locate it.

Financial Management

Now for the fun stuff. Not many entrepreneurs enjoy the number-crunching and bean-counting part of being a business owner, so we've broken down the steps for you in hopes of making the process a little less painful. Basically, your function as a distributor involves paying vendors and collecting payments from customers. The "spread" (or amount that's left over) is your gross profit. In this chapter, we'll show you how to manage that bottom line and handle the bookkeeping issues that most affect wholesale distributors.

For distributors, the biggest challenge is running their businesses on low operating profit margins. Adam Fein of Philadelphia-based Pembroke Consulting Inc. suggests making your operations as efficient as possible and turning inventory around as quickly as possible. "These are the keys to making money as a wholesale distributor," he says.

And while the operating profit margins may be low for distributors, Fein says the projected growth of the industry is quite optimistic. In 2012, total sales of wholesaler-distributors reached $4.9 trillion, and for 2013 the NAW expects that number to grow by an estimated 6 percent.

Playing the Markup Game

In its most basic form, wholesale distribution is all about the "spread," or profit margin, between what you bought the product for and what you sold it for. The bigger the spread, the bigger the profits. For example, in the wine business, Alexandria, Virginia-based Borvin Beverage achieves a 30 percent profit margin. People place great value on high-end wines, so they're willing to pay more for bottles of chardonnay than they will for, say, computer modems. At YogaFit Inc. in Los Angeles, California, Beth Shaw says she strives for a 50 percent markup on all goods. That means the yoga mat that she buys from a supplier for $20 will be sold to her customer for $30.

Laura Benson, owner and founder of Jeanne Beatrice, LLC, in Minneapolis, Minnesota says she had early struggles with markup. "I was unfamiliar with the concept of buying and selling wholesale and to retail outlets," says Benson, who enlisted the help of her local SCORE office for that any various other business challenges. Using a mix of that advice plus trial and error, she now adds up her cost for a single basket—plus freight and any other additional charges—and doubles that number to come up with a wholesale price. "That's the bare minimum," says Benson. "So if someone is buying an item at $5, then the selling price has to be $10 for wholesale—if not higher, in my opinion."

Distributors can use the following formula when it comes to markup: If it costs the manufacturer $5 to produce the product and they have a 100 percent markup, then you (the distributor) buy it for $10. Following the same formula, the wholesaler would double the cost and

Beware!
Don't assume that just because your company is located in a rural location that you can gouge customers with high prices. These are the days of the educated consumer. Remember that your customers are using the web to obtain product and pricing information with just a few clicks of the mouse.

Standard Balance Sheet

The Industrial Supply Association recommends using the following standard balance sheet to figure out your company's net worth:

Assets

All Current Assets

    Cash

    Accounts receivable

    Notes receivable

    Inventory (as reported on federal tax return)

    LIFO reserve

    Other current assets (including prepaid expenses such as catalog, insurance, and interest)

All Fixed Assets

    Real estate (appraisal or cost)

    Land

    Land improvements

    Building and improvements

    Machinery, furniture, vehicles, office equipment, etc.

Other Fixed Assets

    Investments at cost or market

    Other assets

Total Assets:

Liabilities

All Current Liabilities

    Accounts payable

    Notes payable (include current portion of long-term debt and short-term bank loans)

    Federal and state income tax payable

    Payroll deductions

    Accrued expenses (salaries, commissions, sales taxes, payroll taxes, profit sharing, mortgage payable, etc.)

    Other current liabilities

All Long-Term Liabilities

    Long-term debt (including mortgage)

    Total Liabilities (current and long-term):

To figure your company's net worth, subtract your liabilities from your assets:

Standard Chart of Accounts

The Industrial Supply Association recommends using the following standard chart of operating accounts.

Goods Sold

1. Company sales: _____
   (including stock sales, special order sales, direct shipment sales, service shop sales, and returns and allowances)
2. Cost of goods sold: _____
   (including cost of stock sales, special order sales, direct shipment sales, and service sales)
3. Subtract line 2 from line 1: _____

Operating Expenses

4. Selling expenses: _____
   (includes outside sales and sales administration expenses, inside sales expenses, purchasing expenses, delivery expenses, land and building occupancy expenses, warehouse and service shop operating expenses, office expenses, administrative and general expenses, data processing expenses, labor expenses, and other expenses involved with running your company)

Other Income and Deductions

5. Other income: _____
   (includes cash discounts earned, commissions or rebates, income from investments, and miscellaneous income)
6. Other deductions: _____
   (includes cash discounts allowed, interest on borrowed money, loss on sales of capital assets, and loss from bad debts)

Net Profit Before Taxes

7. Add lines 3 and 5: _____
8. Add lines 4 and 6: _____
9. Subtract line 8 from line 7: _____
   (This is your company's net profit before taxes.)

Less Taxes on Income

10. Federal taxes on income: _____
11. State taxes on income: _____
12. Total income taxes: _____

Net Profit (or Loss) for the Year

13. Subtract line 12 from line 9: _____

sell it for $20. Thus, there is a 400 percent markup from manufactured price to the wholesaler's customer.

Managing Your Cash Flow

When you step back and look at the way the money flows in the manufacturer-distributor-customer relationship, it's not hard to see that the person in the middle may end up dealing with some special issues when it comes to cash flow. With manufacturers asking for payment and customers asking for extensions, the distributor can wind up feeling a bit squeezed at times.

The good news is that there are ways around it: by being judicious about your collections, thorough with your customer credit checks, and miserly when negotiating terms with suppliers. By taking these steps, you'll be able to more effectively manage the all-important "cash flow" in your business—a particularly important point for new distributors. Another good way to manage cash flow is to always thoroughly screen all new buyers carefully before extending credit to them. Remember that while most of these firms won't have an official Dun & Bradstreet rating to access, you can use the internet, local banks, current customers, or other resources to learn as much as you can about a firm's viability. Finally, be sure to ask for references on your credit application and call them to see what others will share about their experiences working with that particular company.

The same process holds true on the other side of the coin—where you ask for credit from your vendors. For new distributors who want a positive cash flow, setting up strong credit relationships with vendors is a must. That way, you can turn around and offer credit to your own customers and avoid carrying too much risk on either side of the equation. To make that happen, not only do you need the financial relationships that allow you to purchase products, but you also need those that allow you to extend credit to those customers who want to purchase products from you.

Tax Issues to Consider

While there are few things that distributors need to do differently from any other business in terms of filing state and federal income taxes, sales tax is a sticky area that every distributor must be aware of.

When it comes to collecting sales tax, the real challenge lies in determining which of your customers are tax-exempt and which are not. Generally, if your customer is reselling products to an end user, that customer is tax-exempt. Schools and religious organizations are also usually tax-exempt. However, you cannot take their word for it because ultimately, the responsibility will fall on your shoulders to collect from those who should be paying.

As you go about your business as a wholesale distributor, you're going to encounter companies that are tax-exempt and those that are not. This is a particularly important point to pay attention to, since neglecting to collect sales tax from those that aren't exempt can result in you having to pay back taxes plus a penalty from the Department of Revenue. And don't take the customer's word for it—if they are exempt, have them fill out a tax-exempt form, write their tax-exempt number on it, and sign it. As a distributor, you are responsible for collecting the appropriate forms, but customers that falsify

Dollar Stretcher

Instead of calling all over the place to look for state-specific information on sales tax, check out your state's Department of Revenue website online. Find the appropriate site by keying the words "Department of Revenue and (your state)" into search engines like Google (www.google.com) or Yahoo! (www.yahoo.com).

information are held accountable for their actions (the company is covered as long as the form is on file). The bottom line is this: be judicious about collecting and paying your sales tax, and about maintaining a good file or database of completed forms from customers that don't have to pay sales tax. That way, you'll be covered if a sales tax audit rears its ugly head.

When figuring out the profitability of your new company, it's always handy to have the numbers in a chart format for easy access and comparison. The Industrial Supply Association (ISA) has broken that information down into two charts: a standard balance sheet (see page 79), which compares expenses vs. income to figure out your company's net worth and a standard chart of accounts (see page 80), which lists most categories that a wholesale distributor uses. According to the ISA, distributors in need of more detailed financial records can establish their own subgroupings within the listed categories.

In the last chapter, we'll give you some terrific tips and inspirational stories (and a few words of warning) from entrepreneurs who have already gotten their feet wet in the wholesale distribution business and want to share their expertise with you.

Learning from the Pros

Let's face it: Everyone wants to be successful, and there's nothing quite like starting your own business to enrich your life personally and financially. Sometimes, however, the road from start to finish is a bumpy one. The first two years of your wholesale distributorship's existence will be the

▲

"learning" years, when you experience the ups and downs of being a new business owner in a new industry.

On the positive side, plenty of wholesale distributors came before you and are now overflowing with advice and inspiration that will help you reach your goals. Here are a few thoughts to keep you going through the startup phase.

Managing the Credit Game

Because every wholesaler plays the middleman position between manufacturer and distributor, the real challenge lies in leveraging that position to your best advantage. While it may appear that you're powerless being stuck between the two, there's also a

The Selection Process

As a new wholesale distributor, one of the first questions you'll have to ask yourself is: What am I going to sell? There are many different answers to that question. Maybe you've had a great business idea germinating inside your head for years—just waiting to come out. Or, perhaps you have a specific passion or interest that you feel would translate well in the wholesale distribution market. Or perhaps you've picked up on a market need that you feel you can fulfill by starting up your own wholesale distribution business. Regardless of the impetus behind your idea, be sure to select something that you enjoy doing and that you can really sink your teeth into—something that you care about that you really want to do (not that you just have to do). By taking an introspective look at your personality, likes, dislikes, and interests before you hang out your new shingle, the odds that you'll achieve your goal will be much higher. As an added bonus, you'll love getting out of bed in the morning to put time and effort into your new business.

"Small businesses can consume a lot of time and energy, so make sure you pick something that you really like doing and that energizes you," advises serial entrepreneur Pat Sullivan, CEO at software developer Contatta in Scottsdale, Arizona, and author of *10 Things Every Successful Entrepreneur Needs to Know*. Once you've narrowed down your choices, take the time to learn everything you can about the business, the industry as a whole, and the customers you'll be serving. "Do the due diligence before you jump into it," says Sullivan. "That will help you determine the long-term potential of your idea and whether it's right for you."

"glass is half-full" way to look at the relationship. As a wholesale distributor, it's up to you to make the other two businesses work in sync: You're helping the manufacturer get its products to market, and you're helping the customer obtain the products he or she needs to run a business.

While playing that important role, one of the major mistakes a wholesale distributor should avoid at all costs is the overextension of credit to customers. This tends to occur when one or more of your customers demands extended payment terms on their invoices, yet your manufacturers are demanding their own payment terms on the other end. You can avoid this by being diligent about checking credit references, meticulous when explaining your payment terms to new customers, and careful about not letting your receivables become too old, or "aged."

> **Tip...**
>
> **Smart Tip**
>
> When it comes to spelling out your payment terms, be sure to put it in writing for new customers and then give them a copy. Should they try to back out of paying you on time, you can remind them of the terms they agreed to when the relationship started.

The other part of the credit issue is the customer who buys too much and leaves you "overexposed" (meaning one particular customer owes too large of a percentage of your receivables). You can avoid this by setting an appropriate credit limit upfront, then reviewing the customer's account on a twice-yearly basis (or whatever time frame works best for you). Credit limits can then be increased based on the customer's payment history.

Clearing the Hurdles

In any business, the obstacles to success are many. Fortunately, we all learn from our mistakes, so each new challenge usually leaves entrepreneurs smarter and more seasoned.

At Los Angeles, California-based YogaFit Inc., Beth Shaw says one of her firm's biggest challenges is minimizing the time between receipt of a customer order and receipt of the goods from the manufacturer or supplier. "Not getting product from our suppliers on time is a constant challenge," says Shaw, whose firm stocks inventory, but also relies on timely shipments from suppliers, particularly on popular items that her customers buy in bulk. To work through it, Shaw not only pressures suppliers to fulfill orders faster, but also provides realistic time frames (such as "allow two to four weeks for delivery") to customers.

To guarantee that those customers are well taken care of in the interim—and on all future orders—Shaw says she impresses on her staff the importance of impeccable customer service. "I really drill it into our staff, teaching them how to handle both satisfied and difficult customers," says Shaw. "We also teach them how not to let people steal their time and how to address their needs and solve their problems in an efficient manner."

Good Advice to Heed

In the business world, advice for startups is rampant but not always sound. Also, not all of it applies across the board, so what's good for the wholesale distributor may not be so good for, say, the manufacturer of widgets. For this reason, we've distilled a few important tidbits of advice from the wholesale distributors and experts we interviewed for this book. Here's what they had to say.

Laura Benson, owner and founder of Jeanne Beatrice, LLC, in Minneapolis, Minneapolis, advises both new and growing distributors to pay attention to consumer tastes and buying shifts—both of which can quickly derail even the best laid business plans. "Keep tabs on economic changes, what people are willing to spend, and other trends that could significantly impact your business," says Benson. She adds that knowing what your strengths and weaknesses are—and then rounding out those attributes with either in-house or outsourced support/help—goes a long way in helping businesses get off of the ground and stay in growth mode. "I don't think you need to know all the answers at the beginning, so just trust that if you know you're ideas

Swing Low, Sweet Liabilities

When Keith Schwartz launched his Ohio-based wholesale distributorship, he started small, investing a mere $700 in inventory and starting from the corner of his living room. His startup funds were spent on a bunch of closeout men's belts and ties, bought directly from the manufacturer and sold to a 13-store chain of Drug Emporiums.

"They put them in their store for Christmas, and they sold. In fact, they flew out the door," says Schwartz. Seeing the ties and belts sell so well led Schwartz to believe that he had a viable business idea on his hands. The year was 1991, and he slowly grew the company from his living room to his basement to his garage. Finally, when it was absolutely necessary, he rented some pallet space in someone else's warehouse on which to store his products. Because he doesn't believe in unnecessary liabilities, Schwartz waited until the last possible minute to lease his own space.

Bright Idea

If you're looking for solid examples of entrepreneurs in action, check out the trade magazine or journal for your new industry. Most include at least one real-life profile story in every issue. For example, someone getting into the beverage industry might flip through *Beverage Digest* or *Beverage World* for inspiration and information.

good, it probably is," say~ was one baby step at a tir it, I was selling baskets."

Evan Money, presid Rancho Palos Verdes, in today's tech-oriented tomers can find new sources ᴏ the simple click of a mouse—relau remain a strong foundational element of any distributor-customer transaction. "As the world gets larger, it really gets smaller and flatter," Money explains. "So while someone can do a deal direct with a distributor in China or India, the reality is that the customer may never hear from that source again once they've paid for the merchandise," says Money, who has heard multiple horror stories along those lines from customers over the last few years. "Rather than focusing on being the low-price leader, put an effort into building strong relationships. That energy will be well spent over the long run."

According to Adam Fein, the new challenges currently facing wholesale distributors will also generate new opportunities for the companies working in the industry. "Wholesale distribution has survived by continuously reinventing itself," he says. "Today's entrepreneurial wholesaler-distributors are putting themselves on the road to profits by becoming suppliers of customized and differentiated relationships throughout the supply chain. The wholesale distribution industry will continue to survive and thrive by building on its long history of reinvention and innovation."

Now that you have the soup-to-nuts view of what it takes to start a wholesale distribution business, we know you'll go out there and knock 'em dead. Be sure to check out this book's Appendix—which lists the phone numbers, addresses, and websites of important contacts—and the glossary, for a view of industry-related terms you'll probably know by heart within a few months.

Good luck!

Beware!

Advice is nice, but don't believe everything you hear! Take every piece of advice and information you get with a grain of salt. For example, if a competitor says his or her startup period was so rough that he or she almost didn't make it, remember that they may be trying to dissuade you from coming into their market.

Appendix
Wholesale Distribution Resources

Getting your feet wet in a new industry can be daunting at times. For this reason, we suggest enlisting as much help as you can get (preferably free!) from industry organizations, business consultants who specialize in a particular field, and the vast number of books and other publications available on the market. Of course, the trick is to filter through and find out which of those resources can truly be of help and which ones can be a hindrance to your company's success. While we couldn't list every available resource, we chose to concentrate on those that would most help the new wholesale distributor find business startup assistance.

Associations and Professional Organizations

Alabama Wholesale Distributors Association, 600 Vestavia Pkwy., #220, Birmingham, AL 35216, (205) 823-8544, fax: (205) 823-5146

American Wholesale Marketers Association, 2750 Prosperity Ave., #530, Fairfax, VA 22031, (703) 208-3358, fax: (703) 573-5738, www.awmanet.org

California Distributors Association, 1215 K St., Ste. 1450, Sacramento, CA 95814, (916) 446-7841, fax: (916) 442-596

Colorado Association of Distributors, 15532 E. Kenyon Ave., Aurora, CO 80013, (303) 809-3731, fax: (303) 952-7752

General Merchandise Distributors Council, 1275 Lake Plaza Dr., Colorado Springs, CO 80906, (719) 576-4260, fax: (719) 576-2661

Idaho Wholesale Marketers Association, P.O. Box 953, Boise, ID 83701, (208) 342-8900, fax: (208) 342-8949

Industrial Supply Association, 100 N. 20th St., 4th floor, Philadelphia, PA 19103, (215) 320-3862, fax: (215) 564-2175, www.isapartners.org

Mississippi Wholesale Distributors Association, 5125 Old Canton Road, Suite 203, Jackson, MS 39211; (601) 957-1849; fax: (601) 957-0293

National Association of Wholesaler-Distributors, 1325 G Street NW, Washington, DC 20006, (202) 872-0885, fax: (202) 785-0586, www.naw.org, email: naw@nawd.org

North Carolina Wholesalers Association, P.O. Box 2012, Raleigh, NC 27602, fax (919) 834-8447

Southern Association of Wholesale Distributors, Georgetown Square, Suite C, 3459, Lawrenceville Suwanee Rd., Suwanee, GA 30024, (770) 932-5810, fax: (770) 932-3276, www.the-southern.org

Texas Association of Wholesale Distributors, 8100 Shoal Creek Blvd., #100, Austin, TX 78757-8061, (512) 346-6912, fax: (512) 346-6915

Virginia Wholesalers & Distributors Association, 4900 Augusta Ave., #101, Richmond, VA 23230, (804) 254-9170, fax: (804) 355-8986

West Virginia Wholesalers Association, 2006 Kanawha Blvd., Charleston, WV 25311, (304) 205-5496, fax: (304) 343-5810

Books

Integrated Distribution Management: Competing on Customer Service, Time, and Cost, Christopher Gopal and Harold Cypress, Business One Irwin/APICS Library of Integrated Resource Management)

Facing the Forces of Change: The Road to Opportunity, Adam J. Fein, Pembroke Consulting, www.pembrokeconsulting.com

Managing Channels of Distribution: The Marketing Executive's Complete Guide, Kenneth Rolnicki, American Management Association

The Complete Distribution Handbook, Timothy Van Mieghem, Prentice Hall

Wholesale Distribution Channels: New Insights and Perspectives, Bert Rosenbloom, ed., Haworth Press

Consultants and Experts

Channel Marketing Group, David Gordon, 12520 Ribbongrass Ct, Raleigh, NC 27614, www.channelmkt.com, email: dgordon@channelmkt.com

Doba, Brandon Delgrosso, 1530 Technology Way, Orem, UT, (801) 765-6000, www.doba.com

Lindenwood Associates, Nat Wasserstein, 328 North Broadway, 2nd Floor, Upper Nyack, NY, (845) 398-9825, nat@lindenwoodassociates.com

Pembroke Consulting Inc., Adam Fein, 1515 Market St., Suite 960, Philadelphia, PA 19102, (215) 523-5700, fax: (215) 523-5758, www.pembroke-consulting.com

Market Research

Industrial Market Information Inc., Tom Gale, 2569 Park Lane, Suite 200, Lafayette, CO 80026, 1-877-224-9677, info@imidata.com, www.imidata.com

Publications

Industrial Distribution, 199 East Badger Road, Suite 101, Madison, WI 53713 www.inddist.com

Modern Distribution Management, 2569 Park Lane, Suite 200, Lafayette, CO 80026, www.mdm.com

Successful Wholesale Distributors

Borvin Beverage, Don Mikovch, 1022 King St., Alexandria, VA 22314, (703) 683-9463, fax: (703) 836-6654, www.borvinbeverage.com, email: dmikovch@borvin-beverage.com

Extreme Sports, Evan Money, Rancho Palos Verdes, CA, (310) 750-6219, www.evan-moneyleadership.com

Jeanne Beatrice, LLC, Laura Benson, Minneapolis, MN, (612) 564-5523, laura@jean-nebeatrice.com

Nicole Brayden Gifts and Divinity Boutique, Keith Schwartz, 31225 Bainbridge Road, Suite I, Solon, Ohio, (216) 581-9933, www.nicolebraydengifts.com

YogaFit Inc., Beth Shaw, Los Angeles, CA 90277, (888) 786-3111, www.yogafit.com

Glossary

Alliance: an agreement in which two or more companies team up to increase their buying power or increase efficiency within their firms.

Back-end activities: those activities that go on behind the scenes, like warehouse setup and organization, shipping and receiving, and customer service.

Broker: someone who facilitates the transfer of materials between manufacturer and customer but generally doesn't hold inventory.

Build-out: modifying the interior of a location to meet your company's needs.

Business-to-business: a method of doing business in which a company sells to other companies and not to end users.

Consolidation: a trend in which companies either buy one another or merge with one another to increase efficiency.

Cost per thousand (CPM): when buying advertising (media), this refers to the cost it takes to reach 1,000 people.

Direct sales: when a manufacturer bypasses the distribution channel and sells directly to the end user.

Distribution channel: a way of distributing goods that finds products moving from manufacturer to distributor to end user.

Drop-ship: a shipping method in which a manufacturer ships directly to a distributor's customer.

Durable goods: products that can be used repeatedly (office equipment, furniture, etc.).

End user: the person or entity that will ultimately use a manufactured product.

Fill rate: the rate at which a company fills customer orders.

First in, first out (FIFO): an accounting system used to value inventory for tax purposes.

Free on board (FOB): a common shipping term that means the price of the goods covers transportation to the port of shipment and the usual loading charges.

GAF: general merchandise, apparel, and furniture.

Inventory: the amount of product that a distributor stores in a warehouse or other facility.

Lots: preferred quantities (usually large) of a certain product that a manufacturer wants to ship to a distributor or end user.

Markup: the amount of money distributors add to their cost before selling to their own customers.

Nondurable goods: products with a predetermined life span (writing paper, groceries, etc.).

Payment terms: the number of days between the shipment of an item or items and the date an invoice is due to be paid.

Rack merchandising: displaying products for sale on self-service display racks in retail stores.

Reseller: a company that buys product from a manufacturer and sells it to another company, who will then sell it to an end user.

Return on investment (ROI): a profitability measure used to gauge the earning power of the owner's total equity in the business.

Spread: the amount of money left over after a product has been sold and the vendor has been paid.

Standard industry classification (SIC): a method of classifying industries using definitions from the SIC manual.

Stock-keeping unit (SKU): a term used to define each item stocked in a warehouse or store.

Supply chain: the product and information flow that encompasses all parties, beginning with a manufacturer's suppliers and ending with the end user.

Warehouse manager: the employee ultimately responsible for the smooth running of a distribution facility.

Index